Roland 'Roly' Sussex is Emeritus Professor of Applied Language Studies at The University of Queensland and has been broadcasting language segments on ABC Radio in Queensland every week for 23 years (and in South Australia for 20 years). Since his formal role at The University of Queensland finished in 2010, he has been actively involved not only in the written and electronic media, but also in supervising research at the university, and in undertaking research projects, especially on pain and communication, and intercultural communication.

He has chaired the Board of the State Library of Queensland and the Alliance Française of Brisbane, and is currently President of the English Speaking Union (Queensland).

WORD FOR TODAY

ROLY SUSSEX

UQP

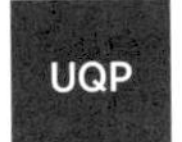

First published 2020 by University of Queensland Press
PO Box 6042, St Lucia, Queensland 4067 Australia

uqp.com.au
reception@uqp.uq.edu.au

Copyright © Roland Sussex 2020
The moral rights of the author have been asserted.

This book is copyright. Except for private study, research, criticism or reviews, as permitted under the *Copyright Act*, no part of this book may be reproduced, stored in a retrieval system, or transmitted in any form or by any means without prior written permission. Enquiries should be made to the publisher.

Cover design by Jo Hunt
Illustrations by John Eyley
Author photograph by Geoff Cavanagh
Typeset in 12pt Berkeley Oldstyle Book by Jo Hunt
Printed in Australia by McPherson's Printing Group

This project is supported by the Queensland Government through Arts Queensland.

The University of Queensland Press is assisted by the Australian Government through the Australia Council, its arts funding and advisory body.

A catalogue record for this book is available from the National Library of Australia.

ISBN 978 0 7022 6306 4 (pbk)
ISBN 978 0 7022 6461 0 (epdf)
ISBN 978 0 7022 6462 7 (epub)
ISBN 978 0 7022 6463 4 (kindle)

University of Queensland Press uses papers that are natural, renewable and recyclable products made from wood grown in well-managed forests and other controlled sources. The logging and manufacturing processes conform to the environmental regulations of the country of origin.

UQP is not responsible for content found on non-UQP websites.

CONTENTS

INTRODUCTION

In June 2014, a deeply disruptive idea struck Kelly Higgins-Devine, the presenter of my weekly language talkback program on ABC Radio Brisbane.

'Why don't you do some short pieces on language?' she asked innocently. 'Current topics, odd words – that sort of thing. They could be broadcast at various times during the day and might attract listeners to the language program.'

At that stage, the language program had been running for half an hour every week for 17 years. Perhaps we needed something new, some reinvention.

'That sounds interesting,' I said, cautiously but innocently. 'Let me do a couple of trial scripts to see how they might work.'

And thus was born 'Word for Today'. I have written and recorded nearly 700 of these pieces, at a rate of two to three per week, over six years. I write and record them in blocks of 10 or so in the promo studios at the ABC in Brisbane, under the rigorous eye and ear of Geoff Cavanagh. Geoff's approach is gentle, disarming and anything but innocent. 'You're sounding very flat today,' he might say. Or, 'That one's too long. You need to lose 30 per cent.' Or, 'Those paragraphs don't hang together. Don't you think you'd better rewrite them?' Or, 'Those words just don't run nicely in a phrase. Can you put them in a different order?'

Geoff is invariably right. I take his advice without demur or argument, and he then processes each piece with his advanced audio skills. Each file is put on the ABC's internal database for programs and presenters to use as they see fit. Some ABC presenters interstate have seen fit, especially in the Northern Territory.

My colleagues at the ABC quickly spotted an opportunity, not at all innocently, and christened these pieces WfT – not, if you please, WtF – and out of that I did my innocent part in coining the new word *wooftie*. Not the most elegant neologism of English, but it is slowly gaining traction in usage, at least in Queensland.

These 'Word for Today' pieces range right across the spectrum of English, including its history. Sometimes they pick up a new usage, or a new misusage. And wherever I go I am, more or less innocently, harvesting data. If you find someone with a notebook and pencil behind a display shelf in a supermarket, that's probably me collecting more examples of real live English in use from shoppers arguing over vegetables.

This makes the 'Word for Today' pieces sound haphazard and scattergun in their approach, and I was initially happy to let them proceed in that way. But, about six months after they started going to air, I began to get requests: 'When are you going to turn those things into a book?' Friends, family members and confidants have been bending my ear to this effect with increasing intensity. So I finally sat down to consider the heap of woofties.

It turned out that they have some recurring themes. A particularly rich vein of topics concerns the origins of words, their forms and their uses, otherwise known as etymology. Did you know that the word *salary* comes from the Latin *sal* for 'salt', since part of the payment to Roman soldiers was in salt? Or that the word *snorkel* began life in a German submarine and is related to the German word for 'snoring'?

Then there are new words, technically known as neologisms. English is growing at an amazing rate, and in order to talk about our rapidly changing world, our language has to try to keep pace. A lot of these, like *TL;DR*, spring up in social media and our digital communications. *TL;DR*, as you will discover, means 'too long; didn't read'. Which is a trifle obscure, but nonetheless *impactful* (there is another new word).

English also re-uses existing words in new ways. Some of these have the same effect on me as shingles would, if I had shingles. I do not react positively to people *reaching out* to me, in order to *engage with* me.

If English is showing bouncing creativity in making new words and uses, it is also profligate in misuses and mistakes. For instance, the Latin phrase *carpe diem*, made famous in the film *Dead Poets' Society*, does not mean 'seize the day' – the scriptwriters got that wrong – but something like 'cherish the day', which is more gentle and reflective. Then there is the problem of pairs of words like *adverse* and *averse*, which are often, and sometimes catastrophically, confused. Or you can travel interstate and find the locals speaking a different language. In South Australia, patients in a hospital are not wheeled around on a *gurney*; they use the word *barouche*, which was originally a four-wheeled horse-drawn carriage. Presumably patients in South Australia must move faster than elsewhere.

Cutting across these categories there are oddities, like the astronomical word *syzygy*, or unpredictable combinations of words, like *laying a tackle* in Australian rules football. And sometimes I allow my mind to wander, as in the suggestion that we should have a new word for the speed of the wind based on the walking pace of a wombat. Keep an eye out for these weird entries, which are framed with borders in this book.

So that is how *Word for Today* came about. These pieces all reflect an idea that has driven my language radio programs, in Queensland for 23 years and in South Australia for 20 years. I was taught English at school as if it were inert and locked down – a closed set of rules to be obeyed and implemented in what we wrote and read. But English is far more than that. It has become the world language, spoken to varying degrees by possibly two billion people. And it is extraordinarily, richly and excitingly creative. The ferment that is modern English is entirely consistent with the idea that it does indeed have rules and traditions that we need to know about, and here I am a cheerful traditionalist. But we also need to wonder and try to understand what is happening in contemporary English, and where it might be going.

Join *Word for Today* and experience the world of English.

Etymology and Origins

BUY SALT WITH YOUR SALARY

Our salary is what we earn. It comes from the Latin word for 'salt', which is *sal*.

So how did salt become dollars?

Roman soldiers were paid a *salarium*, which was money to buy salt. Or (we can't be sure) they may have been paid partly in salt. Or both. In those days, salt was a precious and valued commodity. This gave rise to the Anglo–French word *salarie*, which is how it arrived in English long after we bothered about buying salt with our earnings.

Next time you pocket your salary, remember that you're worth your salt. Which is to say, your *salary*. You've earned it.

GENITAL WITNESS

The Latin word *testis* means 'witness'. This is the source of English words like *testify* and *testament,* which involve a witness. Latin *testis* also means 'testicle', as it does in modern medical English. The *-cl-* part of the word in English comes from a Latin diminutive suffix, meaning a 'mini-testis'.

How did it come about that a single word has two such strikingly different meanings?

There is a story that the Ancient Romans would swear on their testicles. The courtroom TV would have had some memorable close-ups. Only men could do this; women were disqualified from swearing: (a) by their social position in Ancient Rome; and (b) by being testicularly unequipped.

This charming story is almost certainly a folk etymology. If etymology is the study of the history of words and phrases, then folk etymologies are popular beliefs about word origins that seem plausible, but are not borne out by historical evidence. The real story of *testis* is probably more abstruse.

In Classical Greek, the word *parastases* meant 'witness' (*para-* meaning 'alongside' and *sta-* being the root of the verb 'stand' – someone standing by). In its dual form – the grammatical form for 'two of a thing' – the idea of 'things side by side' was transferred to testicles.

Now shift some centuries later to Latin. Historically in Latin the word *testis*, meaning 'witness', came from *tr-* meaning 'three' and *sta* meaning 'standing'. So someone, a third person, standing by as witness to a transaction or undertaking. Since the Romans copied many things from the Greeks, they took the idea of 'standing by' as in *witness* to 'standing alongside' as in *testis*.

This parallelism of forms and meanings involving witnesses and testicles is unlikely to be a coincidence. According to authoritative etymological sources, this is probably how the Latin word came to have two such disparate meanings. English borrowed both, but with the 'testicle' meaning of *testis* accompanied by the diminutive suffix *-cl-*.

One more for the road: the regular Greek word for a single testicle was *orkhis*, hence the modern English word *orchid*, from the shape of the tuber. One would almost think English had a preoccupation with the prurient.

AVOCADO

Here's another twist on confused etymologies and testicles: beware the avocado. The word *avocado* has been confused etymologically with the Spanish word for 'lawyer' (think of 'advocate', in modern Spanish *abogado*; the Spanish for *avocado* is now *aguacate*). The term for the fruit reached English via Spanish – remember that the Spaniards were early explorers in Central America – together with exotic stories about lawyers and avocados. But lawyers are a folk etymology here too. The Spanish word *avocado* for the fruit actually came from a mishearing of an Aztec (more accurately: Nahuatl) word *ahuacatl* meaning 'testicle'. For proof, just hold a *Persea gratissima* up to the light and consider its profile.

If you have a score to settle, think of *ahuacatl* next time you sink a knife into a Hass or a Fuerte.

SYZYGY

English has some words that look improbable. One of the weirder examples is *syzygy*, which means a conjunction or opposition of planets and heavenly bodies in a line, especially of the sun and moon: 'This month they will be in syzygy'. It comes from a Greek word meaning 'yoked together'.

Remember that the next time you are playing Scrabble™ and can put a *Z* on a triple word score. But you will need a blank for the third *Y*, since Scrabble™ provides you with only two.

This reminds me of a perennial question about the letter *y*. Is it a vowel or a consonant? The answer is that when it comes before another vowel it functions as a consonant: *yes*, *yard*, *your*. Elsewhere, it's a vowel: *by*, *fly*. It can also make diphthongs (a sound consisting of a glide from one vowel to another) after another vowel: *boy*, *clay*. *Y* is something of a chameleon.

USQUEBAUGH

There is – I am not pulling your leg – a word in English that begins with the letters *usq-*.

It is *usquebaugh*. Look it up in the dictionary. If you don't find it, look it up in a bigger dictionary. The word is English. Just.

Usquebaugh comes from the Celtic languages, including Irish and Scots, which we sometimes call Gay-lik but that are also pronounced Gah-lik or Gallic. Or, if you really know your language from your limbic system, *THE Gaelic*.

Usquebaugh is an Anglicised version. It comes from two Celtic words: Scottish *uisge*, pronounced ish-kuh, meaning 'water'; and *beatha*, pronounced ba-ha, meaning 'life'. So *usquebaugh* means 'water of life'. That sounds evocative and poetic. It is, in a way, because if you go back to the Celtic word for water, or ish-kuh, you may guess that *usquebaugh* means 'whisky'.

Whisky is made from fermented and distilled malted grain. *Whisky* has two spellings, with and without the *e*. The Irish and Americans write it with an *e*. The Scots, and after them the rest of the world, leave the *e* out. Which is what you should do if you fear the wrath of the Scots.

MOONDAY TO SUNDAY

Our names for days of the week are so familiar that we seldom stop to reflect on what they really mean. Or really meant, long ago.

Monday to *Sunday* is actually *Moon-day* to *Sun-day*. All very astronomical.

Saturn takes us back to the Roman god of agriculture, and gave us *Saturday* – a day of gardening and weeds.

Tuesday to *Thursday* are all old Norse and old Germanic. *Tuesday* is the day of Tiw, the Germanic god of war and the sky. Do not choose Tuesday to make peace with anyone. *Wednesday* is the day of Woden, the supreme Norse god. Don't mess with anyone on Woden's day. *Thursday* is the day of Thor, the god of thunder. We might have thought of that.

Only one of the days of the week is feminine: *Friday*, or Frigg's day. She is a Norse goddess of love, and the wife of Woden.

This is all very convenient when we email *TGIF*, or 'thank God it's Friday', to a colleague, and the colleague responds with *POETS*, or 'push off early, tomorrow's Saturday'. And we push.

Just as well we named the days of the week as we did.

FLOWER AND FLOUR

As any semiliterate person in English knows, the two words *flour* and *flower* are pronounced identically. One makes bread; the other is botanical, displays pretty colours on a plant and attracts pollinators. But even the fluently literate may not know that the two words come from the same source.

The story goes like this: the source is the Latin root *flor-* for 'flower', the thing that grows on a plant. *Flor* gave us words like *floral* and *florid*.

We borrowed the Latin word *flor* through French, and it quickly established two forms: one more like the French source – *flour* – and one following English patterns with a *w* – *flower*. Both were used for parts of plants and for the ground wheatmeal used to make bread. The *flour* version, however, was also used to refer to the best part of the ground wheatmeal, which is a sense we have retained today in slightly poetic phrases like *the flower of his youth*. And, since English is English, that idiom uses the *w* spelling.

In the early nineteenth century, the confusion was

sorted out by assigning the *w* spelling to plants, and the *flour* version to bread making.

So, if you make your best beloved a loaf of bread from the finest ground wheatmeal, you are using the flour of the flour for someone in the full radiant flower of their beauty. And you should buy a bunch of flowers as well, in case the bread doesn't rise properly.

LUNAR AND LUNATIC

Why should we expect lunatics to be crazy once a month, roughly speaking?

It's all the fault of Latin, and the French who borrowed the idea, and it's our fault for borrowing it in turn from the French.

The word *lunatic* derives from the Latin word *luna* for 'moon'. According to medical belief and superstition from the early centuries of the Common Era until about 1700, the phases of the moon caused temporary and intermittent insanity. The moon was also associated with epileptic fits and various forms of mental disorders and disturbances.

In modern times, if you are feeling erratic, you can claim to be *moonstruck*. That may not cut the mustard with your employer, partner, family or friends, but you will have the best part of two millennia of medical superstition to back you up.

TIRAMISU AS A PICK-ME-UP

A *pick-me-up* is a drink or food that makes you feel better, especially if you are feeling down, seedy, hungover, jaded, flat or depressed. It gives you renewed energy and zip.

Hangovers are probably the commonest reasons for requiring a pick-me-up. Among the pick-me-ups for hangovers are coffee, eggs, broth, massive rehydration like a parched camel, and more alcohol.

But there is a simpler, sweeter, milder answer: *tiramisu*. Some think that this word is Japanese, but it's Italian. Tiramisu consists of layers of sponge flavoured with coffee, cocoa, egg, sugar and mascarpone. Some add an alcohol like Marsala. The Italian verb *tirare*, meaning 'pull', has an imperative form *tira*; *mi* is 'me'; and *su*, among other things, means 'up'. Taken together, *tiramisu* means – literally, really literally – 'pull me up'.

Italians eat tiramisu as a dessert. A good tiramisu after a large meal does give one a feeling of being picked up, even airborne. The height you reach may depend on the amount of Marsala added.

RESTAURANT

In French, *restaurant* originally meant 'restoring'. The French verb *restaurer* means 'to restore', and a *restaurant* was a place where you went to restore yourself by eating something. In the mid-eighteenth century, restaurants were especially for poorer people and served dishes like fortifying soups. No Michelin three stars for restaurants in those days.

The word *restaurant* is now a noun in English and French and many other languages. You go there to eat food prepared on the premises, sometimes food of great sophistication and even greater cost.

The next time you feel peckish, consider restoring yourself from the fridge. It will almost certainly be much cheaper, faster and more convenient.

While we are on the topic of restaurants, the person who owns such a restoring establishment is not a *restauraNteur* but a *restaurateur.* Do not make this mistake if you have pretensions to being a connoisseur of food. In French, someone who 'restores' others with food and drink, a 'restorer', is a *restaurateur*. In contrast, *restauraNteur* is an English *faux pas* combining the noun *restaurant* and the suffix *-eur.* Definitely not worth a single Michelin star.

JERUSALEM ARTICHOKE

Some phrases use familiar words, but when we look closer we find that they are based on mistakes.

Such a phrase is *Jerusalem artichoke*. We know what *Jerusalem* is, and where, and we know *artichoke*, an edible flower of a plant whose name comes to our tables from Arabic via Spanish and Italian.

That's all fine and dandy, except that a Jerusalem artichoke has nothing to do with Jerusalem. It comes from the Italian *girasole*, which means 'sunflower'. Not Jerusalem at all. Nor artichoke, which is a flower; the part of the Jerusalem artichoke that you eat is the tuber. As is well known, if you've sat in a field of sunflowers during daylight hours, the flowers turn to face the sun. This is what the Italian word means: *gira* from *girare* meaning 'to turn', and *sole* meaning 'sun'. The Americans have got this one right; they call a Jerusalem artichoke a *girasol*.

The Jerusalem artichoke is, at least by name, an impostor. So exact punishment on it next time you bite into one.

DEAD AS A DOORNAIL

The phrase *dead as a doornail* has been in English since about the fourteenth century. It is an echo phrase, where sounds are repeated in different words: *Dead as a Doornail*.

But no-one can agree exactly how it came about.

According to one origin story, when you hammer a doornail into a door it sticks out on the other side. If you then, as carpenters say, *kill* the nail by banging it flat, it can't be pulled back out from the other side, and that makes the nail dead. This sounds plausible, especially because you *kill* the nail. But there isn't enough evidence for us to be conclusively certain.

An even less likely explanation is that a doornail was a metal plate on a door that the striker would hit when you knocked. It would not move, and eventually would be dented, and so dead. But that etymology is even more doubtful.

Be that as it may, it won't stop us from using the phrase. If a living thing, or an idea, is dead as a doornail we might as well phone the undertaker.

HUMDRUM

At first sight, *humdrum* is an odd word. It doesn't improve at second sight either. It means boring and tedious, and it sounds like it.

The origin of *humdrum* is probably the word *hum*, which is itself a dull kind of noise, and the process by which you derive *humdrum* from *hum* is called reduplication. In other words, you copy or repeat the first part of the word, either as a perfect copy or with some modification.

So if you are *shilly-shallying* and *dilly-dallying* about adding another hungry mouth to your family, think carefully of the *pitter-patter* of tiny feet. If you decide to be bold and procreative, don't be a *namby-pamby*. Eschew *argy-bargy*. What you need is a bit of *rumpy-pumpy*. Which could make you feel like the *bee's knees*. That is, until you remember how many *knick-knacks* you have to buy to stock the nursery of the new arrival. You will, after all, have been partaking in personal reduplication, in a manner of speaking.

HEARSE

We tend to use words associated with death in hushed and respectful tones. They are ominous words, and we don't want to provoke the evil spirits.

One such word is *hearse*. Nowadays it means a large formal car or vehicle used to carry bodies from a church or funeral home to a cemetery or crematorium. It's a ceremonial vehicle, and usually a fairly posh one, out of respect for the departed. A hearse could not be Bruce's rusty old ute. Well, not normally.

But a hearse was not always a vehicle. The word *hearse* originally referred to a plough-like ancient harrow. Then it was transferred to a triangular frame for holding candles in church services. And then it became a frame over a coffin to support hanging drapes and similar ornaments.

Eventually the word *hearse* came to be used for the carriage used to carry the coffin. To take the ashes and dust back to the earth where they began, and where the hearse began as a harrow.

FOUR LEGS AND FLIES

Puns are fun. They may be the lowest form of wit – a claim that dates from the eighteenth century and is at least as old as Dryden the poet and Johnson the writer of dictionaries. They may be, in the words of Ambrose Bierce, 'the form of wit, to which wise men stoop and fools aspire'. But they are still fun.

Puns depend on words having two or more meanings, like *this year's flu is going viral*. Sometimes they depend on something more subtle, when we have to understand a sentence a different way, and the second meaning snaps into view and trips us up.

We can get two for the price of one if we combine puns with riddles.

What has four legs and pants? That sounds as if *pants* is a noun, meaning 'trousers'. But trousers are typically worn by two-legged entities, aka people. So we pause, confused, and then we try again with a different type of sentence. What happens if *pants* is a verb, meaning rapid breathing? And suddenly it's obvious: a dog. Dogs pant.

Now try *what has four legs and flies?* Our first thought here is that *flies* is a verb. Are we dealing with a pig with wings? Most things that fly don't have four legs, with the marginal exception of glider possums. And they don't really fly … So, we recalculate. What happens if *flies* isn't a verb at all, but a noun? Bingo. Any farmyard animal surrounded by flies will do: pigs, cows, horses.

Spurn not the pun. It's kept generations of people making jokes, sometimes feebly, but at least playing with language. Like the candidate at the elections who lost their seat and won't be able to stand until the next one.

STEAL MY THUNDER

Why would we want to *steal someone's thunder*? There's nothing much you can do with it once you've stolen it, and its only value is as a statistic for the Bureau of Meteorology. Once it has done its thunderous thing, of course.

The story behind the phrase to *steal someone's thunder* goes back to the theatre in London around 1709. A dramatist called John Dennis had written a tragedy called *Appius and Virginia*, which must have been tragically bad, because the season was extremely short. However, Dennis had also invented a new way of doing stage thunder, and that is about the only feature of his play that has survived.

And been imitated.

Shortly after the failure of his own play, Dennis attended a performance of *Macbeth*, which had truly impressive thunder. HIS thunder. The story goes that he sprang to his feet and cried, 'Damn them! [...] They will not let my play run, but they steal my thunder'.

If you would like to be dramatically immortal, the

next time you write a blockbuster screenplay make sure you include really superlative stage effects. The screenplay may fizzle and die, but your effects will outlive you.

LIMELIGHT

Being *in the limelight* is something that happens to celebrities. And, from time to time, to politicians, sometimes in ways that are not so welcome.

So where do you go to buy some limelight?

Before the advent of electricity, lighting a theatre stage was a major problem. Candles and gas gave only a modest amount of light, and you needed a lot for decent illumination, which created a fire hazard.

But in 1816, a British scientist called Thomas Drummond discovered that burning lime – in other words, calcium oxide – in a jet of hydrogen and oxygen would produce a brilliant white light. These lights began to be used in the theatre in 1837 and were called *limes*. At last the actors could be seen. The lights had to be constantly supervised if they were to keep working uniformly. But, after all, the play's the thing.

The parts of the stage that were lit in this way were usually centre and front, and from that we get the notion of an actor being illuminated in prominent public view. But that meaning of *limelight* – being in the public eye, irrespective of artificial illumination – isn't actually recorded until 1902. Since then, we have developed much more stable ways of generating large amounts of light, and lime is no longer used for theatre lighting. However, the propensity for actors, artists and public figures to seek the limelight, and hog it, has grown exponentially.

BLUE MURDER

Why should we scream *blue murder*? What is blue about it?

Blue murder is an example of English sucking in language material from all across the map. In this case – as has happened so often – the source is French.

In French, the word for *God* is *Dieu*. Until recently, the French had the same taboos as we do about uttering the name of the deity with disrespect. English speakers avoid saying *God* by using words like *golly*. These avoidance expressions are called *euphemisms*. Or, in the case of blasphemy and obscenity, *minced oaths*.

There was a French expression *Mort Dieu*, literally 'death God'. The French changed that to *morbleu*, which literally translated means 'death blue'. The English seem to have picked up the blue part, and turned death into murder. And of course the French have the expression *sacré bleu*, originally *sacré Dieu* or 'holy God', which they changed for safety and propriety into 'holy blue'.

This seems to be a long and winding explanation, but the *Oxford English Dictionary* supports it. *Blue murder* is only used for shouting loudly: *screaming blue murder*.

Once we had *blue murder*, we moved on to blue in different senses. To be in a *blue funk* or *blue fear*, for example, is to show extreme cowardice or to be extremely scared. All of which has nothing to do with *having the blues* or *playing the blues*. Except a chance similarity of sounds.

AMBULANCE

The word *ambulance* comes to us from French. At the beginning of the nineteenth century, the French invented a mobile hospital cart, drawn by horses, which went to the wounded rather than waiting for the wounded to be taken to the hospital. This vehicle was called a *hôpital ambulant*, or 'walking hospital', and the *ambulant* part is indeed related to our verb *to amble*, meaning to go for a walk.

In the French expression, the word *ambulance* derives from an adjective and modifies the word *hôpital*. A more natural way to turn this into English would have been to invent the phrase *mobile hospital*.

But, over time, the ambulance became a vehicle with a different role. It still went to the sick or wounded, but then took them to the hospital. And once it acquired internal combustion, it certainly was not ambulant anymore, but rapidly mobile, with a siren. The original idea of walking persists in the name, but it is no longer a very accurate description of how the vehicle gets around.

Other languages have solved this naming problem in a more logical way. In German, an ambulance is a *Krankenwagen*, or a 'sick persons' vehicle'. In Russian, it is *skoraja pomoshch'* (скорая помощь) or 'fast help'.

And the French? They now have *ambulance*, as we do. They invented the idea and gave it to us, and we gave it back.

If you have to call for one, be grateful that it's faster than ambulant.

BANTAM

Have you ever wondered why chickens and boxers are both called *bantams*?

The word *bantam* comes from the name of a province in Java, Indonesia. Bantam chooks were thought to be imported from there in the nineteenth century, although in fact they do not come from Bantam in the first place. This is an illegitimate example of an eponym – a word named after a person or place, like *sandwich* or *wellington boots*.

Back to bantams. From the behaviour of the chook, which is small, ferocious and quick moving, we have applied the word to a particular group of boxers, specifically between 51 and 54 kilograms.

So the next time you see a bantamweight bout in the ring, hark back to the heroic cocks who gave their name to this aspect of the noble sport.

But there is a further twist to the tale. English even got the spelling wrong. The province in Java is spelt *Banten*. If you care about the integrity of placenames, it's enough to ruffle your feathers.

TRIVET

You probably know the word *rivet*. But what about *trivet*?

Nowadays a *trivet* is a board or protective pad – a heat mat – which you put on a table to stop hot containers from burning or scarring the surface. But originally a *trivet* was something quite different.

Trivet used to mean a tripod that stood over a fire to put a kettle or pan on. Or a hook over the fire to hang a kettle or pan on. Or a stand with three or more legs. The British even have the saying *as right as a trivet*, which means to be in raw good health. Though I am still trying to work out why a blackened metal support is a good point of comparison for one's wellbeing.

The word *trivet* starts with *tri-*, which is where the idea of 'three' comes from. Indeed, *trivet* probably derives from the Latin root *tripes-*, meaning 'three-footed', which we know as a tripod.

Modern trivets have lost any connection with 'three', except for the prefix *tri-*. Perhaps we should try to use heat mats in threes – partly to protect wooden tables, but also to reassure them that their origins aren't forgotten.

SNORKEL

For most of us, a *snorkel* is a tube for breathing under water when we swim with a face mask. In modern English, *snorkel* is also a verb: you can *snorkel* or *go snorkelling*.

But the snorkel actually began life in submarines, as a tube that allowed a submarine to get air from the surface while submerged. This tube was a German invention in the 1940s.

The derivation of the word *snorkel* is rather more colourful than that. In German, it's called a *Schnorchel*. And in German navy slang *Schnorchel*, meaning 'nose' or 'snout', is related to the splendidly onomatopoeic word *schnarchen*, meaning 'to snore', to which it is indeed historically related. Apparently the submarine snorkel sounded like a U-boat snoring through a nightmare under water. By all accounts, the sound was loud, disagreeable and off-putting. But, as any swimmer will tell you, if you need air, you need air.

If you were a swimmer waiting for the invention of the snorkel to go with your face mask, your desire would have been fulfilled around 1951. Before that, the snorkel was just for submarines. Complete with sound effects.

SHARPSHOOTER

A *sharpshooter* is someone who is very accurate at shooting with a gun, usually a rifle, since pistols and other such handguns are not very accurate.

There is a belief that the term *sharpshooter* came from the name of the Sharps rifle. In America in 1848 an inventor called Christian Sharps took out a patent for a rifle, which became famous for its accuracy, especially in the American Civil War. The Sharps rifle was a breech-loader, and was much easier to use and reload than the older muzzle-loading rifles. The idea was that a person who was a dead-eye dick with a rifle was a sharpshooter because they had a Sharps rifle.

Unfortunately, this is a folk etymology. The origin from the Sharps rifle sounds feasible, because there were certainly sharpshooters in the American Civil War, and many of them used Sharps rifles. However, the earliest recorded use of the term *sharpshooter* is around 1800, almost 50 years before Christian Sharps took out his patent.

The easiest way to test folk etymologies is by the date. In this case, the earliest sharpshooters did not have the benefit of Christian Sharps' patented gun.

FALL PREGNANT

Until about the middle of last century, it was not considered polite to talk directly about pregnancy. The word *pregnant* itself was thought to be indelicate. If this vital biological condition was discussed at all, people said things like *in an interesting condition* or *in the family way*.

Nowadays pregnancy, pregnancy tests and pregnant women (and animals) are right across the airwaves, television and the internet.

But one unusual phrase persists: *to fall pregnant*. When we use the verb *to fall* with a following adjective, it tends to refer to something undesirable that happens against our will: we *fall sick*, for instance. So why should we talk about the continuation of the race as if it were like undesirable and unfortunate events?

One answer lies in the history of English. In the eighteenth century, *to fall* meant 'to become pregnant': 'They were married eight months before she fell'.

But why don't we say *falling* when we talk about animals *in the family way*? We say 'The cat IS pregnant', or 'The cat GOT pregnant'. Cats and dogs and whales and gorillas don't *fall pregnant*.

Perhaps we should stop saying *fall pregnant* entirely. *Become pregnant*, or even *get pregnant*, is much nicer. Or, if you know your Latin roots, *become gravid.*

COLD TURKEY

The word *turkey* was originally a shortened form of *turkey cock*, and was applied to the guineafowl that reached Europe through Turkey. Then someone applied the name to the American bird – biologically something very different – which is how the gobblers of this world came to the dinner table.

The word *turkey* – not the country – has some negative meanings. A film that flops is a *turkey*, and someone who is acting in an inept or incompetent way is a *turkey*: 'They caught me painting graffiti on the wall and I felt like a complete turkey'.

Turkeys aren't supposed to be rocket scientists, either. A stupid or self-defeating action is *like turkeys voting for Christmas*, like casting a vote for your own roasting.

But there is a more favourable side to *turkey*. To *talk turkey* is an American phrase meaning to express yourself frankly, to stop *beating about the bush* and *get down to brass tacks*.

There is also the odder phrase *cold turkey*, meaning

to do something abruptly and decisively, especially giving up a habit like smoking or drinking or doing drugs. Some have compared the *cold* part to the clammy skins of those in withdrawal. A more likely source is the *talking turkey* phrase, where *turkey* relates to concrete, decisive action.

Let us assume, for the sake of argument, that you don't want to look like a turkey. Your partner is banging on, talking turkey about you quitting your addiction to quinoa cold turkey. You wisely take the safer route and make an appointment with a quinoa therapist.

SCRUB MULLET

Before the days of refrigeration and air transport, food supplies in Australia were much more seasonal and local. You ate what could be caught or grown in your neck of the woods at that time, unless it was preserved, salted or dried.

Particularly during the Depression years in the 1930s, many foods were not available or could not be afforded. As a result, housewives – in those days this burden fell overwhelmingly on them – had to dream up ways of using what they had to imitate what they hadn't.

This led to dozens of recipes with the word *mock*, indicating that the contents weren't quite what the name suggested. There was *mock fish* and *mock chicken*, both of which never came within a country mile of either seafood or chook. The recipes can still be found in old Red Cross and CWA cookbooks of the period.

A listener sent me one I hadn't heard of: *scrub mullet*. A mullet is a sea fish not easily accessible in the scrub, or the bush. But in outback Australia in the 1930s there was a lot of lamb. A side of lamb would be consumed from the roast down, as it were. After a few days, what was left would be cut into thick slices, dipped in batter and fried. And that was called *scrub mullet*.

Colonial goose was also made from lamb, this time from boned, rolled and stuffed shoulder or flaps. This was genuine heroism in the kitchen. The name and the image were there to overcome the absence of the real thing.

Next time you complain that the freezer is empty, pause and reflect on the fate of our forebears. They had no freezer. But there was lamb all the way to the horizon. One might almost say a *lambscape*.

SAYINGS OF YESTERYEAR

Older speakers of English in Australia, including me, often lament the disappearance of many lovely sayings that have either died or are on their last lexical legs.

Expressions like *they'd even pinch the holes out of your socks* are striking and original. Apart from the cheerful lack of logic, pinching the holes out of someone's socks denotes a really mean person. That's almost as bad as saying that someone would *steal the milk out of your tea*. Technically difficult (without some rather advanced and very modern equipment) but, in terms of social ethics, a hole in one.

We also used to say something was *so weak it couldn't pull the skin off your custard*, or an unwell person could be *coughing like a rat in a chaff bag*.

My grandmother was very proper in speech. Her generation considered it indelicate to refer directly to having had enough to eat, let alone too much. She would say that she was *full up to pussy's bow* or, on another day, *full up to dolly's wax*. Has anyone seen a wax doll recently?

GOOGOL AND GOOGLE

The name of the ubiquitous search engine Google is actually and deliberately a corruption of another word.

That word is *googol*, which is defined as the number 10 raised to the power of 100, or 1 followed by 100 zeroes. The idea was that the search engine Google would be dealing in very large volumes of digital stuff. The term *googol* was invented in 1920 by Milton Sirotta, who was a nephew of the mathematician Edward Kasner.

The search engine Google was originally named *BackRub*. Founders Larry Page and Sergey Brin were right to make the change. You wouldn't want to *backrub* a football score.

Neologisms

SCIENTIST

The word *scientist* is very common in modern English.

But *scientist* is a neologism – a new or invented word. It dates from as recently as 1834, when it was proposed at a meeting of the British Association for the Advancement of Science. It first occurred formally in print in 1840, in a book called *The Philosophy of the Inductive Sciences* by the Reverend William Whewell. As he put it, there was a need for a word 'to describe a cultivator of science in general' to replace the then-current word *philosopher*.

The word *scientist* didn't become widely accepted until the end of the nineteenth century. There was a long-running controversy over which bits of knowledge were covered by this new term.

This also poses a problem for the Scientific Revolution, which is commonly agreed to have begun in 1543 with the publication of *De revolutionibus orbium coelestium* ('On the revolutions of the heavenly spheres') by Nicolaus Copernicus (in his native Polish, Mikołaj Kopernik). Copernicus placed the sun, not the earth, at the centre of the universe. He was a scientist, though he didn't know that yet. He'd have called himself a philosopher.

TRENDING

If you spend a lot of time on the web, you will have noticed the word *trending*. You may well have been overwhelmed by it.

Trend started out as a noun: a 'tendency'. Now it's often used as a verb, and *trending* in its new definition means something like 'to gather momentum'.

To begin with, things *trended upwards*: 'The housing market is trending upwards'. Now things just *trend*. YouTube™ has a *trending feed*. If you have aspirations of coiffure you can search for *trending hairstyles*.

Most trends occur in the Twitterverse, where *trending hashtags* are used a lot. I have even heard of a *trending field of study*: a field that should soon be worthy of our attention.

It all makes me ponder: if a trending trend can only trend upwards, what happens when the trend runs out of steam and starts to describe a downwards trajectory? Is that an *untrend*?

WOMBATS

If you are on a boat or a plane, you measure your speed in *knots*. Not *knots per hour*, which is wrong in the same way that an *ATM Machine* is wrong. A *knot* is a measure of speed in itself.

Kilometres – and *miles*, remember them? – are measures of distance. So if you want to specify your speed in kilometres you have to say *per hour* after it: 'A wind of 17 kilometres per hour'. What a mouthful.

We need something shorter, and Australian, since no ordinary person knows how fast a knot is. I have a suggestion.

Wombats walk at about 1 kilometre per hour. I have walked with wombats, and this is a reasonable average. So let's have a new measure of speed: the *wombat*. The weather people can say, 'The wind is 17 wombats'.

How elegant. How short. How Australian.

I need your help. Recommend the wombat as a measure of speed to all your friends, work colleagues and politicians. Then we can change the speed regulations: not 60 kilometres an hour, but 60 wombats. It would have wider applications: 'He did 136 wombats in a 60 wombat zone and lost his licence'.

WI-FI

The term *Wi-Fi*, usually spelt with a capital *W* and *F* and a hyphen in the middle, is now so common that we don't even realise that we don't know what the term really means.

Hi-fi is easy: it stands for 'high fidelity' and has been in use since the 1950s to refer to recorded sound of particularly high quality and fidelity.

Wi-Fi dates from around 1999, though there is some doubt about its birthday. The name was coined by a brand-consulting firm in the United States called Interbrand Corporation.

Wi-Fi (or *Wifi*) refers to a LAN or 'Local Area Network', typically with a radius of around 20 metres or so within a house, and rather more in the open air. Many restaurants, shops, enterprises and even cities are now providing free Wi-Fi as a means of attracting customers. You can even connect to Wi-Fi on a plane at 35,000 feet. The traveller's last haven free from Wi-Fi is shrinking. *Sic transit pax mundi* ('there goes the peace of the world').

All that still hasn't solved the origin of the name. *Wi-* obviously stands for 'wireless', a network where you do not need to plug a physical lead into a box to make it work.

But where does the *Fi* part come from? It does not stand for 'wireless fidelity', which would make it parallel to *hi-fi* and 'high fidelity'. The best guess – and for something as vital to our personal and professional lives as Wi-Fi, this is very unsatisfactory – seems to be that the term *Wi-Fi* is a variation on *hi-fi*. The *Fi* part was assumed, but actually left undefined.

Can you have *Wi-* without the *Fi*? Who knows? Talking about a LAN just doesn't make the grade. When we are out and about we look for the Wi-Fi logo, with those radiating transmission lines from an imaginary aerial. Our digital device makes contact. And we are fulfilled. We have Wi; who cares about the Fi?

TROLL

In folklore, a *troll* was an ugly creature that lived in a cave or under a bridge and threatened people. Trolls were either giants or dwarfs, and all the trolls that I have ever read about were male (when they did in fact show any gender characteristics).

Nowadays a *troll* is someone who deliberately makes nasty, insulting or provocative comments about another person or people online. They can be of any gender. There is a verb too: *to troll*. Both the noun and the verb can be pronounced like either *doll* or *dole*, with my informal survey of university and radio colleagues splitting 50/50. Either way, the word is spelt like the cave-dwelling grump, which is where the term probably originates.

Trolling is the contemporary form of what used to be called *flaming*, but I have the impression that trolling can be even nastier and more personally damaging. Trolling can also be done anonymously. All of which really does suggest internet trolls disseminating their ominous messages from dark, dank, bat-filled caverns.

Over the 20 years or so since flaming channels were the rage, the internet has refined its ability to grief people. *To grief people?* Good grief. And I don't mean Charlie Brown and *Peanuts*.

GHOSTING

Dating, that useful word that we avidly borrowed from the Americans, is fraught with pitfalls. And that's without the intervention of dating websites, which offer more or less explicitly a variety of encounters from the platonic to the romantic and well beyond.

The digital element is important in modern dating. Rather than telephoning or speaking to someone in person, we can make assignations via instant messaging channels. These channels are fast, convenient and cheap. And, with the exception of hackers and the occasional security disaster when your intimate details are broadcast for all to wonder at, they are reasonably secure.

Online messages are also very useful when we want to butt out of whatever connection we have developed. You just stop responding to messages. You ignore enquiries asking, 'Are you still there?' You don't answer entreaties, blandishments or threats. You become a black hole in the internet.

There is even a term for this act of falling silent:

ghosting. You become the person who isn't there, insubstantial and invisible.

If simply being silent is too much for you, there is help at hand. There is a company that will, for a suitable fee, contact the other party and inform them that you are no longer connected. Their services range from sending emails to cards (physical or virtual), digital gifts and cookies. This is more than unfriending. This is terminal separation. Your internet ghost becomes a spectre.

TL;DR

The volume and energy of internet communications have given rise to a wide range of new expressions. Many of these are primarily written rather than spoken. If they are spoken, they are often initialisms, which means that we pronounce them as letters: *BTW* is 'by the way'. But if they contain a vowel we can also try to pronounce them as words: *ROFL*, meaning 'rolling on the floor laughing', is either 'R-O-F-L' or 'rofle', to rhyme with *waffle*.

Some of these initialisms can have subtly differing implications.

TL;DR means 'too long; didn't read'. It contains four letters with a semicolon in the middle. It is one of the few internet initialisms with punctuation. The semicolon isn't pronounced, except as a brief pause, but the letters are. We have created a new variety of silent letter, in a manner of speaking. Not that we usually express punctuation like that, with the possible exception of the American *period*, as in 'That's all I'm going to say, period'.

TL;DR is most common in blogs and online discussions when one of the participants has a long and self-indulgent rant, and other participants decline to read it on the grounds of length. They add *TL;DR* to the blog as a means of protest.

But *TL;DR* also has a second meaning. Sometimes a reader (or the writer) takes pity on other readers and provides a shorter, précis version of the offendingly long paragraphs. And that précis is headed by *TL;DR*. This time it means, by implication, 'the original was too long to read, here's a shorter version for convenience'.

We had better stop now, before someone rejects this 'TL;DR' as TL;DR.

FRIEND ZONE

You may know the phrase *friend zone,* which refers to a platonic relationship – friendly, relaxed, uncomplicated and with no sexual overtones or undertones, implications, expectations, entanglements, ramifications or innuendo between two people.

There are even websites with earnest advice about how to avoid the friend zone. Or, if you find yourself stuck in the friend zone, advice on how to get out of it and advance a relationship into more hormonal pastures.

The word *zone* itself implies a defined area with designated behaviour. The term *friend* is usually positive. But the phrase *friend zone* defines a limitation: that's as far as you are going to go.

Even more devastating to barely born amorous aspirations is when you turn the phrase into a verb: 'I feel really bad that I friendzoned her, but I had to do it'. If you are friendzoned by the object of your hopes and – more relevantly – desires, then you are pushed out of passion's way and into amiable but less exciting territory.

It could be worse. A hopelessly amorous panting young swain could be *acquaintance zoned*. Or even *unfriendzoned*, aka *rejected*.

FOMO

Most of the acronyms and initialisms generated by social media are light-hearted, casual and irreverent. I am thinking of *LOL* for 'laughing out loud' or *RTFM* for 'read the owner's [expletive substituted] manual'. Or, more pointedly, *PEBKAC* for 'problem exists between keyboard and chair', aka you, and you alone. Human error.

But a few of these acronyms are less superficial. One such acronym is *FOMO* for 'fear of missing out'. You exhibit FOMO when you stay connected to your social media all the time in order to be present when and if anything happens. Or might happen. FOMO is also a fear of regret that something will happen when you aren't there.

FOMO itself has escaped the thrall of social media, and is found in everyday life. In compulsive investors, for instance, who cannot bear to turn off the Bloomberg financial TV feed, and sit in front of their screens, watching minute fluctuations in the value of the dollar.

We talk about FOMO as if it's a disease. You suffer

from FOMO, have a case of FOMO, are unable to shake off FOMO.

We could try to counteract FOMO with another acronym: *MO;TH* for 'missed out; thank heavens'. The end of angst, the start of a new relationship with your loved ones and breakfast with nary a screen in sight. Oh, liberation! Or we could have a global halt on social media for a day. If only we could afford the FOMO.

CATFISHING, HATFISHING AND SOCKPUPPETS

You probably know what a catfish is, but have you ever been *catfishing*? Without a boat or rod or bait, at least metaphorically?

It all has to do with social media and personal relationships. If you engage in catfishing, you create a false image of yourself to ensnare the interest of another person online. The false persona that you create is called a *sockpuppet* (usually just one word) since the outer appearance of the sockpuppet may not be consistent with what the hand inside the puppet is like.

You can even be catfished if you fall for someone else's sockpuppet and end up madly infatuated with an impersonation.

Especially if you are male, and sensitive about an increasing thinness of hair, you can also *hatfish*, which is a special subcategory of catfishing. You wear a hat all the time, with some pretence about introducing a new fashion. If your hatfish is a plausible catfish, you may achieve some measure of success, at the expense of verisimilitude.

Things were simpler once. You turned up to a date, took off your hat, kissed the lady's hand, offered flowers, bowed to her parents, and drove your Chevy to the levee. No socks or puppets or catfish in sight.

GAMIFICATION

English is currently in the middle of what must be its fastest and most explosive growth ever, especially in vocabulary. Some of these new arrivals are ugly. Some are useful. And some are both ugly and useful.

I rate *gamification* in this last category. The word is ugly, but the only obvious alternative – *gameisation* – is even worse.

Gamification means casting a problem, often a learning task, in a format more like a game, and often specifically a computer or online game. The user is encouraged to take a more active and involved role, so they interact with the things to be learnt in a lifelike simulation. There is competition. There are challenges and rewards, including points, levels of achievement and hierarchies of expertise.

For instance, take Angry Birds. This is a well-known game for mobile devices. You compete to hit targets and score points. Imagine applying that idea to learning French verbs, confronting levels of increasingly difficult and grammatically misshapen French sentences. If it's done well it can be motivating, engrossing, fun and effective. Certainly better than learning hundreds of conjugations parrot-fashion.

For the time being, *gamification* is one of the hottest tools on the block for making learning attractive. Expect to see it in all kinds of contexts that formerly were more prosaic.

DOXING

I recently came across a sinister new verb generated by activities online: *to dox*.

Doxing has nothing to do with *doxy*, an archaic term for a prostitute or mistress. *Dox* comes from *documents*. You take the first syllable – *doc* – and add *s* to make it plural. Then you spell the last two letters with an *x*, which is another internetism. In a similar spirit, think of *tix* for 'tickets' and *pix* for 'pictures', not to mention *pax* for 'passengers'.

If you dox someone, you publish documents in order to reveal personal details about them, sometimes when they have been posting material anonymously and you would like to make their identity public. The details you publish can include their name, phone number, email address, postal address, credit card numbers … Where you stop depends on how devilish or malicious you are feeling, and what the provocation might have been.

Doxing someone can be in retaliation, paying them back for an insult or action that you didn't like. But it can also be purely vicarious, part of the haphazard hurtfulness that so easily happens online, particularly when you can do this anonymously and get away with it.

CUSHIONING

These days, countless numbers of social relationships begin online, through social media sites, dedicated dating websites and dating apps. These services provide opportunities to meet people you would otherwise never encounter in your humdrum everyday existence.

But online dating has its pitfalls and risks. People may not describe themselves truthfully. It's not a great strategy to commit yourself closely to someone until you really know them well. And when you meet them face to face, they can turn out to be fireballs or cold-boiled cabbage, in which case you will have lost a lot of precious dating time, if not more.

A prudent strategy is to have more than one on the string at a time as an insurance policy while you check out the credentials of the latest contact. This approach is called *cushioning*, so that if you do shoot yourself in the emotional foot you have a backup cushion already primed and waiting.

Of course, your backup may be using you as a cushion too. That's the way the cushion crumbles.

KPI >> KQI

Some phrases are made to be hated. Or perhaps they are born innocent and virginal, and we ruin them by misuse and abuse.

Such a phrase is *KPI* for *Key Performance Indicator*. KPIs are the factors that say whether you have achieved what you are trying to do, usually in your job, and they are overwhelmingly quantitative, expressed in numbers: 'You've missed your KPI by 11.317 per cent'.

Turning life into numbers sounds objective and methodical. It's actually nothing of the kind. The figures are as rubbery as the indicators they purport to measure. We fool ourselves egregiously if we think we have a concrete measure of achievement in KPIs.

I have a better alternative: *KQI* for *Key* ***Quality*** *Indicators*. Out with numbers; in with values. Let's see what achievement is really about. I challenge the HR gurus to work on a way of describing the quality of achievement. When you are done, let me know. Otherwise I'll run a KPI on your failure to achieve a KQI, and you will be hoist with your own numerical petard.

DECUMULATE

A listener reported what was to him a new word from a financial report: *decumulate*. It was new to me too.

But we can work out easily enough what it means. To *accumulate* something is to collect it incrementally, to make an increasing heap of whatever it is. You accumulate money, wealth, friends, tulip bulbs, compost and debts. Things can accumulate intransitively as well: 'My compost is accumulating nicely in anticipation of the planting season'.

Accumulate comes from the Latin *cumulus*, which means a 'heap'. *Cumulus clouds* look like heaps and can accumulate cumulatively in the afternoon sky.

So *decumulate* means disposing of, or dispersing, your accumulated heap. To unheap the heap. You won't find the word in most dictionaries, since it's new and rather specialised to the financial area. But at least one bank is reported to have a *Decumulation Department*. So that's where they do what they do with our superannuation. As in, 'My super is being inexplicably decumulated'.

JUST

Just is a deceptive word. If you use it properly you can defuse potentially explosive situations.

Imagine that you are waiting on a report from a colleague. It's late, you are planning Act 1 of Armageddon, but the colleague is older and more senior and prone to gout and choler. So:

Where is your report?

won't do. You can soften that with a question:

Is your report ready?

Still expect an explosion. Try again:

I am wondering if your report is ready.

Not bad. But, even more subtle,

I'm just wondering if your report might be ready.

And with a pretty little ping it appears in your email inbox.

ENGAGE

There was a time, not so long ago, when the word *engage* was most commonly used when two people plighted their troth with the goal of matrimony or holy wedlock, with or without the holes. The word was always in the form with *-ed*: you were *engaged to be married*. You didn't *engage someone to marry you*, except in the sense of commissioning a cleric to perform the ceremony.

To be sure, there were other senses of *engage*. You could *engage someone in conversation* by *engaging their attention*. You could be *engaged in an enterprise*. You could be *engaged to do a job*, or if you were the boss you could *engage someone* when you hired them. If you had a car with manual gears you could *engage reverse*, and if you were partial to the sport of fencing you could *engage someone in combat*.

But nowadays *engage* is everywhere, particularly in the phrase *engage with*.

Teachers are exhorted to *engage with their students*, politicians *engage with their constituents*, business people *engage with their customers*, coaches *engage with their players*. If this use of *engage with* means anything, it seems to imply *to talk to*, *to communicate with*, or more pompously, *to involve in meaningful conversation or interaction*. It seems to be related to another odious phrase: *to reach out to*. When a telemarketer says that they are reaching out to me, I put them on hold for an hour. One doesn't wish to engage with people who speak like that.

REACH OUT

After accumulating some credit brownie points in the loyalty program of a large company, I received an email from a senior managerial person:

> I wanted to reach out to you as a valued member with an exciting update.

Reach out has been around in English for centuries, but in a more concrete sense of extending a hand. Its modern meaning is more like *to contact*, or *to touch base with* (ugh), or even *to set up a meeting with*. The person reaching out initiates the contact, even if they are the ones trying to find help.

You can reach out to someone to offer them information, as in our loyalty program example. You can also reach out to someone when you need help or advice. Or you can reach out to offer help. There is an additional meaning of 'show a kind and positive attitude by contacting someone'. As in:

> I want you to reach out to Bill and see if you can persuade him to come to the meeting.

The evidence suggests that this is an Americanism, and in America it was substantially promoted by an advertisement from AT&T, the communications and telephone company. The slogan in a 1979 advertisement was: *Reach out and touch someone*. Which AT&T encouraged people to do by calling whomsoever they needed to reach out to. This was part of a campaign to soften the company's image, as it had a dominant position in a competitive market.

But the phrase *reach out* has outlasted its welcome. *Forbes* magazine lists it as one of the most annoying pieces of business jargon. I agree. There is something over-precious about it. It's not just *contacting someone*; the *being nice by contacting them* is now hard to separate from the contact itself.

This is why I don't like a loyalty program reaching out to me to tell me about what new services they are providing. They may contact me. They may tell me something. And that's how I wish them to express it. Otherwise it's not reaching, but retching wretchedly.

DRILL DOWN

Forbes magazine is a good barometer of current business practice. So when *Forbes* offers a phrase as an example of 'Jargon Madness', it's worth paying attention. *Forbes* has condemned phrases like *touch base* or *leverage best practice*. Way to go, *Forbes*. Kill 'em dead.

One of *Forbes*' recent offerings for disapproval is *to drill down*.

Drill down started as a concrete verb. If you are a geologist you drill down to discover what is below.

Drill down was then applied to computing and information science. It meant to go to a greater level of detail, as when clicking on an icon to open the material beneath.

But then *drill down* morphed again. It is now part of management speak. It means to consider a question more deeply and in more detail, to uncover the truth or real meaning.

In principle, metaphors like that are fine. They say something familiar in a new and striking way. But when they start to proliferate uncontrollably all over the wordscape they become irritating clichés. You can drill down into a budget, a policy, an analysis, a shopping list, an argument, a disallowed goal, or a decision to ask for a blueberry muffin.

Enough already. Let's call an end to drilling down. I just hope my dentist doesn't read this.

ONBOARDING

If you move in the rarefied atmosphere of corporate and non-corporate management, you may have become aware of a term for getting new members into their respective positions in organisations or companies. It's not yet in most of the important dictionaries, but it's spreading fast.

New staff members have to be inducted. They have sessions to introduce them to an organisation and how it runs, as well as aspects of their duties and responsibilities. In the past, the word *induction* neatly covered this process. There is an even more technical managerial term: *organisational socialisation*.

But now there is a newer word: *onboarding*. You get people *on board*. This all sounds rather like a jolly sailing club, but it's serious stuff, especially with mobile workforces and people moving into and out of jobs more frequently than they used to.

Onboarding is a noun: it's the name of a process. You take the preposition *on* and the noun *board*, glue them together, and declare it to be a verb: *to onboard*. As in,

'The new team was onboarded last week', or 'Tomorrow I'll be onboarding the new financial officer'.

Making verbs like this isn't new in English: think of *upstaging* someone, or *downsizing* a business. Those two are so familiar that we don't even twitch when we hear them.

I certainly twitch when I hear *onboarding*. But doubtless *onboarding* will inoculate me against itself, and with time and exposure I will onboard new colleagues like everyone else.

TAKEAWAY

Successful neologisms often capture an object or activity in a striking and compact way, using one word where otherwise we'd need several.

Such a word is *takeaway*. It started its recent career around 1960 in reference to food, and is British. This in itself is noteworthy, since the Americans invented most fast food, and most of the vocabulary to go with it.

Takeaway was initially a modifier: a *takeaway* meal, meaning food that is consumed away from the premises where it is prepared. That's why the new word prevailed, especially since we do this so often, and need a short way of talking about it.

Then it morphed into a noun: 'Are we going to have takeaway tonight?'

In America, by the way, it's *takeout*.

Now *takeaway* has morphed again, acquiring a new meaning, this one from management speak. I first heard it as *takeaway message*, meaning information or ideas that you take away from a meeting or class or experience. Now *takeaway* is a noun on its own: 'The big takeaway is that we should cook fresh vegetables at home and eat less takeaway food'.

The option not to take it away is not on the table.

LAWYER UP

'We won't be able to get anything more out of him. He's going to lawyer up.'

If you *lawyer up*, you get yourself a solicitor, legal representation and the protection of professional legal advice. You then decline to discuss your case further until your legal bulldog is present and primed. One assumes that the other side will equally lawyer up, which will leave all the talking to the legal eagles.

The way the phrase *to lawyer up* is constructed is a bit unusual in English. There aren't other professions where you add *up* and turn the whole thing into a verb. You don't *doctor up* when you get yourself medical advice, nor do you *reverend up* if you enlist a spiritual or theological guide.

But adding *up* also implies adding resources to meet a need. You *man up* if you rise to the occasion and show fortitude and resolution. I have not found a politically correct female equivalent yet, but I'm looking. *Stand up and be counted* says something similar.

In Australia *to man up* can also mean to get a number

of people to work together to achieve a goal. As in football, where you gather players to provide effective resistance to one or more players on the opposing team.

That's more like *lawyering up*. Let's have a platoon of them. If we can afford their fees.

PRESENTEEISM

We all know what *absenteeism* is: it's staying away from work or school without a good reason. Being a habitual – or, if you prefer, an habitual – no-show. It also implies someone who avoids doing their duty. A bludger, a whinger, someone who selfishly refuses as a matter of habit to do their bit.

It is less widely known that there is a parallel term when people turn up for work when there is a good reason for them not to do so: when they have a migraine, or the flu, or are distracted by thoughts of sick children at home. This word is also used of people who stay at work longer than is necessary or expected, perhaps because they are feeling insecure about their job and want to make a good impression.

The word is *presenteeism*, meaning to be present when you don't need to be.

If *presenteeism* is the opposite of *absenteeism*, it ought to be positive. But *presenteeism* has negative overtones too. It suggests attendance in excess of expectations, together with the idea that you may not be fully functional, or that you're trying to impress by just being there rather than performing well.

In fact, quite a lot of words that end in *-ism* are pejorative. Think of *ageism*, *sexism* and *alcoholism*.

If you are tempted to exhibit *presenteeism*, it's probably better to stay at home.

HEALTHWASHING AND GREENWASHING

Healthwashing sounds as if it might be part of a personal hygiene routine: wash your hands and avoid getting someone else's flu.

But we have been misled. *Healthwashing* is what companies do when they try to persuade us about the healthy nature of their products, while concealing nefarious components or ingredients.

There is even a related term *pinkwashing*, where a product claims to support cancer research but in fact may contain carcinogens.

Then there is *greenwashing*. *Green* is one of the most rah-rah words in advertising, and implies that something is healthy and environmentally conscious. *Greenwashing*, as you will now be able to guess, means promoting a product as good for the environment when it is anything but.

So *washing* is in fact a form of deception. I was brought up to believe that washing your hands, and especially washing behind your ears for some obscure reason, was a sign of cleanliness, which was next to godliness. I'm afraid that the Lord was looking the other way when someone coined the word *healthwashing*.

PETRICHOR

Australian English has a stellar reputation for creating slang and expressive phrases like *mad as a cut snake*, and we are well known for diminutives like *U-ey* and *Freeo*. We are not known for the creation and propagation of scientific terms, which is why it gives me pleasure to document one that has popped back into media attention.

The word is *petrichor*. It means the smell produced when rain falls on hot dry earth. Its origins, etymologically speaking, are impeccably Greek: *petra* is the Greek for 'stone', and *ichor* is the fluid – blood, or whatever liquid is appropriate – that flows in the veins of the gods. Think of it as 'celestial stone liquid'.

Petrichor was invented in CSIRO in 1964 by an Australian and a British scientist for publication in the prestigious journal *Nature*. And we do need a word for this curious and evocative smell, familiar to anyone in an Australian summer, or an Australian drought. It's not easy to explain the feeling of release and relief evoked by the smell of petrichor to someone from a damp climate like Britain. But in Australia, perhaps with a whiff of ozone from a passing thunderstorm, it can mark the end of a stifling day or a devastating drought.

Talk of this smell makes me nostalgic. I must be a real *petrichorophile*.

SHORTEST AND LONGEST

The shortest English word is *I*, or *a*. Just one letter.

The longest reported English word is a chemical monster. It is the full technical name of a protein called *titin* or *connectin* and is supposed to have no fewer than 189,819 letters. No-one can say it, and at best it's a curiosity. Stick with *titin*. Take refuge in brevity.

For reasonable people like you and me, the longest English word is:

antidisestablishmentarianism (28 letters), meaning 'opposition to the disestablishment (i.e. removal from official status) of the Church of England'.

There are also some made-up words, which aren't fully nostrified in English:

floccinaucinihilipilification (29 letters), which was apparently invented by pupils at Eton College to cover the irregular use of the Latin words *floccus*, *naucum*, *nihilum* and *pilus* (and some others).

supercalifragilisticexpialidocious (34 letters), which means 'very nice'. Mary Poppins has much to answer for, including violation of brevity.

FODMAP

Do you suffer from abdominal pain, gas and bloating? If so, we may be able to help you in your hour of need and distension.

It all has to do with the acronym *FODMAP*.

An acronym is a word composed of initials, like *Qantas*, which stands (or at least stood) for 'Queensland and Northern Territory Aerial Services'. There are hundreds of thousands of acronyms in English. A good acronym is pronounceable, usable, sufficiently well recognised, and conveniently shorter than the full form from which it is derived.

FODMAP is a good example of a really useful acronym, since only specialists can say or remember the full version. *FODMAP* stands for 'fermentable oligosaccharides, disaccharides, monosaccharides and polyols'. The acronym also suggests 'food' plus 'map', so it's doubly helpful.

FODMAP foods are not well digested in the small intestine, so they tend to move down to the large intestine, where they are fermented by bacteria.

Fermentation produces gas. Hence the troublesome pain and bloating. FODMAP foods, or FODMAPs, include wheat, onion, garlic, cabbage, pulses like beans, stone fruits, artificial sweeteners, fructans, fructose and lactose. And more.

This is the point where you need Dr Google, followed by a dietician or a gastro-intestinal specialist. But at least you may know, at the end of that process, that you have a FODMAP sensitivity. And you can both write and pronounce it.

ZINGER

A *zinger* is a witty, caustic comment or phrase – a wisecrack, a sharp remark, a one-liner – designed to say something short, pungent, and often cutting and critical. *Zingers* are put-downs or send-ups. They are deliberately scathing, negative and raw.

Zinger is another Americanism, and a good one. Around 1950, the date of its first entry into the *Oxford English Dictionary*, it meant 'something outstanding'. The 'wisecrack' meaning appeared around 1970.

The word *zinger* is rather specific. *Zingers* are usually both public and political. They are less often the off-the-cuff cutting bon mot in conversation that we might generate after three glasses of good wine. Zingers are premeditated. Winston Churchill was good at them, though most of his zingers antedated the term itself. Of Clement Attlee, he once said: 'A modest man with much to be modest about'.

I rather hope that we have seen the death knell of the zinger as a form of political argument: its nemesis, its coup de grâce, its quietus. Because after a decade characterised by governments running on aphorisms and one-liners, it would be a relief if we were in for a period of conversation and discussion in parliaments.

MAN BUN

Man bun – a hair bun, but on a male – is one of a small but growing number of words and phrases that start with *man-*.

Man bun is more popular than *man bag*, and both are ahead of *mankini* (a kind of male lower abdomen coverage with straps that go around the neck). And, perhaps to go with your *mankini*, there are *mantyhose*.

Then there is *man flu*. This term is problematic because it's pejorative and sexist. It evokes a wimpy, whining, cringing, pitiful male unable to tolerate the symptoms of influenza. There is no *woman flu*, pejorative or otherwise. On behalf of my gender, I stand up and protest. Flu there may be, and there may be varying ways of experiencing it, but *man flu* discriminates on the basis of gender. There are rules and regulations prohibiting such things.

I have similar reservations about *man language*. Apparently, men are faulty and limited communicators, and their restricted language prefers 'tangible', 'concrete' words. I haven't seen any sign of this. I think it may be a conspiracy.

A *man bun* is a bun. Calling it a *man bun* risks infecting it with the pejoratives and limitations of *man flu* and *man language*. I think, on balance, shaving your head might be safer.

MANSPREADING

Here's another new *man-* word, coined especially on the underground railway in America, aka the subway.

The word is *manspreading*. It refers to a bodily posture as practised by males, especially younger males, especially on public transport.

To *manspread*, you need to slide down in your seat and assume a sack-like slouch. You then spread your legs, feet angled out. This takes up space that would otherwise be occupied by multiple standing passengers or even by the seated passenger next to you. It can be comfortable. I've tried it, when there was no-one else on the bus. Initially, I objected to the term *manspreading* as sexist and discriminatory, but then I realised that few women sit like this.

In America, manspreading has been declared antisocial. The New York transport authorities are running ad campaigns against it: *Dude … Stop the Spread, Please. It's a space issue.*

I have a different approach. If there are seats for senior citizens, what about a section for manspreaders?

That way, manspreaders can sit in comfort with people like themselves, and perhaps narrow the breadth of spreading if the space won't accommodate all the legs and angles. A *Manspreading Zone*.

After all, perhaps the freedoms of democracy include the freedom to spread?

MANSPLAINING

Good things come in threes? Here we go with *man-* again. Men are currently having a rough time of things, language-wise.

There are some new terms for men behaving inappropriately in conversations. The behaviours are old, but we suddenly seem to have a need of terms to capture them.

One of these is *manterrupting*, when a man heedlessly and needlessly interrupts a woman. The man may have something to add, or not, but he interrupts anyway.

Then there is *bropropriating*, or taking over a woman's ideas after she has presented them but been virtually ignored.

And now there is *mansplaining*, when a man takes it upon himself to explain something to a woman that the woman already knows, and that may well be something that women would normally know more about than men.

Are we males so inconsiderate? I initially thought not. But, once you are aware of the words, you become aware that the actions they describe are more common than I for one am comfortable with.

I can hear a female voice in my head: ‘Well, actually, Roly, you haven’t got it quite right. A full understanding depends on how men recognise their role in the conversation and their point of view, and their ability to view conversation roles not only from the angle of the speaker, but also of the listener and the bystander ...’

Indeed.

FUR BABY

The word *baby* in English is very ancient and probably derives from an infant's first attempts at speech, or at least using its vocal organs. Without babies our race would not persist. And without the Americans the word *baby* would not have prospered nearly as well as it has. They introduced the words *baby* and *babe*, and more recently *bae*, to describe or address your special friend, lover, boyfriend or girlfriend, or significant other.

There are dozens of phrases and expressions in English involving *baby*. Not only do we have *baby blue* for the *baby boomers*, but one's *baby doll* may be *baby-faced* and engaging in *baby talk* before they try a *baby walker* and dribble over the *baby grand*. We have *cry babies*, and if you *baby* them excessively they may turn into *baby monsters*.

There is a new addition to the list: *fur baby*. This phrase is used especially when people have a pet and lavish on it the sort of affection that others give to young children. It's usually a cat or dog, but also potentially a kangaroo, lizard or goldfish. With or without fur.

So if you turn up at the vet's with an expensive, extra-special tin of kitty fish fillets and gush, 'How is my fur baby this morning?', the vet may turn aside and reach for a tissue for you, and a bucket for them.

BELFIE

In 2013, the *Oxford English Dictionary*'s Word of the Year was *selfie*: a picture of oneself taken by oneself on oneself's mobile phone. The dictionary makers traced it back to an Australian who had taken a self-portrait of his stitched lip after a mishap involving alcohol, falling, and contact between his lip and a stone step.

Before the advent of cameras on mobile phones, taking a picture of yourself required a camera, a tripod and a self-timer. You pressed the button and sprinted into the frame in time for the shutter to work. That is no longer necessary. Now you just hold the phone at arm's length, smirk and snap.

Mobile phone cameras have also made it possible to take pictures of more than just one's modest self. There is a new word, by analogy with *selfie*, if you take a picture of your posterior. It's a *belfie*. This is an example of a blend or portmanteau word (a term that comes from Lewis Carroll's *Through the Looking Glass*), when parts of two words are glued together. For example, *breath* and *analyser* combine to give us *breathalyser*.

The origin of *belfie* could be *bum-selfie*, or more demurely *bottom-selfie*, or for the Americans a *butt-selfie* or even *booty-selfie*. This fad appears to have been 'shaped' in America with Kim Kardashian, and is now an increasingly common feature of image and language.

In addition to *selfies* and *belfies*, you can take a *couplie*: a selfie of you and your significant other or others. And you can buy a *selfie stick* to extend your reach and achieve a wider angle of view.

I prefer to point the camera's lens outwards.

PREPPER

You may be familiar with *preps* or *preppy* people – those who attend or attended elite preparatory schools (usually in America). But *preps* are very different from *preppers* – a new American word for people who used to be called *survivalists. Prepping* is a multi-billion-dollar business.

Preppers prepare for apocalypses and disasters. They build atomic fallout shelters, and stock them with food and water, ammunition and guns, and other useful things to wait out whatever awful event may befall us.

Sometimes they even locate their shelters in other people's countries, like New Zealand, since New Zealand seems to be sufficiently far away from potential apocalypses to have a better chance of survival.

Frankly, the rest of us can only hope that the preppers have prepped in vain. If you judge things by the advertisers, prepping is an activity for the rich. In which case, as Peter Ustinov once said, the meek shall not inherit the benefits of culture. But as the American TV show *Doomsday Preppers* demonstrates, many low-income families are finding ways to prepare for the apocalypse on a budget. This way for the cut-price apocalypse.

KEEPCUP

Some new English words and expressions are a sad reflection on how low we have fallen. Words like *deepfake* (replacing a person's video image with another, using artificial intelligence techniques), for instance, or *fake news* (news consisting of disinformation or hoaxes, or alleged to be such). But every now and again a new term celebrates the fact that we are actually improving.

One such word is *KeepCup*. It is usually written as one word, often with both a capital *K* and a capital *C* (called 'camel case', or 'CamelCase'). This word is an echo phrase, where the two parts share some sounds, a bit like a partial rhyme – *KeePCuP* – which makes it sticky in memory.

A *KeepCup* is the container that you take to a cafe to have it filled with the beverage of your choice. You save the environment another abominable discarded plastic container, and you save yourself something like $0.50. Win-win. And your conscience has a delicious glow. That is a lot of bang for the minor inconvenience of carrying the cup with you.

The new word *KeepCup* contrasts with the phrase *single use*, like the thin plastic bags from the supermarket that we have finally grown out of.

I have started to bend my mind to a word like *KeepCup* for receptacles that hold soft drinks and alcohol. Perhaps something like *CoddleBottle*. I'm still working on it.

MALWARE

The French word *mal* means 'bad' or 'evil'. It turns up in many words that English has borrowed from French, like *malevolent*, *malfunction*, *malodorous*, *maladroit*, *malpractice* and *malnourishment*.

It is not surprising, given such a vigorous and profligate word, that it should find a place in our modern digital world, this time connected to the good old Germanic root *-ware*. In the days before computers we had *hardware*, which consisted of tools and machinery and things you got from the corner hardware store. And *ware* by itself referred to things like pottery and china.

Then computers came along. The programs that run the computer, and the programs that execute applications like word processing, are called *software*. Computer games involving the violent destruction and dismemberment of living beings are charmingly called *splatware*. Software for espionage, state or personal, is called *spyware*. Programs that occupy a lot of space are known as *bloatware*. Unwanted pop-up advertisements are *adware*. *Liveware* refers to real human beings using computers. *Shareware* and *freeware* tell you that you don't have to pay.

Our old friend *mal* is not going to be left out. *Malware*, which is now fully recognised by your spelling checker and mine, refers to bits of computer code that are designed to damage your data, resources, programs and sometimes the computer itself. It can take control of your computer, steal data, review your private information and generally behave in an evil way, which more than justifies its name.

MISANDRIST

English is good at pejorative words, especially words expressing negative emotions about people. Some of them start with the prefix *mis-*, meaning 'bad' or 'wrong', like *misidentify* or *miseducate*.

Among these *mis-* words are *misanthropist* and *misogynist*. A *misanthropist* is someone who hates humankind: *mis-* + *anthropos* (Greek for 'human being'). A *misogynist* is someone who hates women: *mis-* + *gyne-* (the Greek root of the word for 'woman').

It is ominous that *misogynist* is approximately 10 times more common than *misanthropist* online. Why would we talk about hating women 10 times more frequently than hating humankind?

This also raises an additional question: is there a word for a person who does not like men? Thanks to Greek once more, there is: *misandrist*. *Andros* is Greek for 'male person', so a *misandrist* is someone who hates male humans, aka men.

So there you have it, a trinity of dislike: *misogynist*

for hating women, *misandrist* for hating men and *misanthropist* for hating the whole lot.

That's an awful lot of hating. According to the rules of Greek, someone who loves humankind should be an *anthropophile*. The *Oxford English Dictionary* does not list that, nor does my spelling checker. I'm going to add it manually so that there will be a little light of human warmth in the dark digital cavities of my computer.

MISOPHONIA

A colleague has alerted me to a new word – well, new to me. It's *misophonia*.

At first blush, *misophonia* is opaque and obscure. It's almost invisible online, but with a bit of deduction and analogy we can work out what it means.

The first part, *mis-*, is like the *mis-* in *misanthropy* (the hatred of humanity).

The second bit, *phon-*, is the Greek root for sound. The final *-ia* is found in medical conditions like *haemophilia* or *neuralgia*.

So, *misophonia* is the hatred of sound. More precisely, it's a neurological disorder where a sound causes a reaction like anger or fear.

A phone, of course, is also a communications device that controls our lives. There should be a word *mis-phone-ia* for the mistrust and anger generated by our mobile phones when they misfunction, or intrude on our lives, or interrupt a Schubert sonata.

TICK AND FLICK

Most lovers of the English language enjoy a good echo phrase. An echo phrase is like a rhyme, where sounds of one word are repeated in a following word, resulting in a pleasing phrase that is likely to spread, and stick in the mind, and become a feature of everyday usage.

A particularly apposite and popular echo phrase is *tick and flick*. You receive a document (paper or digital), mark something minimal on it, and send it on to the next person in the sequence. Your minimal mark is represented by a tick, and your rapid transmission by the flick. Sometimes your contribution is limited to ticking a box. In this meaning we are now increasingly tending to use the American *check* or *checkmark*. But the need to rhyme *flick* with something is helping to keep *tick* in use.

Will the phrase *tick and flick* be enough to save *tick* from the inroads of the Americanism *check*? In the long term, probably not. But the phrase *tick and flick* is making a small and sterling contribution to keep it alive.

You can give me a tick for that one, at least.

HEPCAT AND HIPSTER

What do *hepcat* and *hipster* have in common?

At first glance, not a lot. But hold on to your seats and let me tell you a story.

Hepcat is American. It denotes a stylish, impressive musician or music groupie in jazz and rock. It combines *hep* and *cat*. *Hep* means – at my age, I hate to use the word – 'cool'. *Hep* is a variant of *hip*, which also means 'cool' or 'intelligent'. And *cat* is the familiar, and now dated, word for a man, a bit like an older form of *dude*. A *hepcat*, then, is musically a very *cool dude* indeed.

So what of *hipster*? In the 1940s, a *hipster* – this is yet another American term – was the same as a *hepcat*: someone who was very much into the music scene, the kind of *cat* one might like to emulate.

Now there is a more modern incarnation of *hipster*. Well, actually, there are two.

One is a style of trousers that fasten at the hips rather than at the waist. Boring.

The other *hipster* refers to trendy people who follow cultural fashions and activities that are a bit outside the current fashionable mainstream. They tend to have tattoos, copious or recherché facial hair, and try to stay ahead of the next wave of what's fashionable. A kind of advance party of hepcats, perhaps?

SQUINCH AND SMIZE

Can you *smize*? Not to mention *squinch*?

Smize is a portmanteau word or blend of *smile* + *eyes*. If you really want to smile, mouths are not enough. Supermodel Tyra Banks invented the term, and there is even an app that can add a *smize* to your photographs.

Squinch, on the other hand, is a blend of *squint* and *pinch*, and is associated with a New York photographer called Peter Hurley. It's a narrowing of the eyes that is supposed to project self-confidence. Squinching is often used in portrait photography, including selfies. I haven't been able to replicate that effect yet, but I'm on the case.

The word *squinch* is actually much older. It first appeared in the sixteenth century, and it refers to the structure, either straight or arched, that supports a superstructure in a square tower, such as a dome.

This *squinch* comes from *scunch*, which comes from *scuncheon*, meaning 'the inner face of a window or door jamb'.

I am off to buy some sandpaper and a sanding block.

I need to sand and paint my scuncheons to bring a broad smize to the faces of visitors to my house.

GLAMPING

Camping, in its purest form, is a swag under the stars, which can be spectacular.

But there are downsides to that variety of camping, including the need to find water for the billy. And the need to remember to pack the billy in the first place. And the small matter of excavating a loo.

All of that is rendered irrelevant by a new variety of camping. It is called *glamping*, which is a blend or portmanteau formed from *glamorous* and *camping*. Glamping gives you the equivalent of a hot-and-cold-running tent. Not to mention, depending on the level of glamping, ensuites, central heating, fresh linen and – who knows? – possibly even a jacuzzi.

The word *glamping* is British and dates from 2005, but the idea is centuries old. Kings at play, Ottoman dignitaries out for a comfortable weekend, and aristocrats and businessmen taking the air in comfort, surrounded by their retinues, have been glamping for many aeons, though they didn't call it that until recently.

As far as I know, the noun *glamping* is the only form of this new word in current English. It sounds odd to make it into a verb and say, 'Arbuthnot glamped last weekend', or 'He glamps whenever the opportunity presents itself', or 'I've heard that this week they're glamping in a sumptuous yurt in Mongolia'.

MINDFULNESS

The word *mindfulness* has been around in English since the sixteenth century. But it's only since 1899, according to the *Oxford English Dictionary*, that it's been common and even fashionable.

It came into special use in English in association with Yoga and Buddhism. It means being aware of the moment, being conscious of yourself and focused on your own thinking, and on yourself doing the thinking. It's an intense state of heightened self-awareness. It can also be liberating and elevating, and can provide feelings of exaltation, or quiet contemplativeness. It's non-judgmental: it sees things as what they are.

In this sense, mindfulness is in strong contrast to the mindless rush of everyday activities, as we load in a task, do it, file it and load in another. Mindfulness is a very un-internet state of being, an unplugged state of mind.

Mindfulness is a serious matter, but in the current climate it also risks becoming a buzzword through overuse and by being made part of trendy therapies and faddish remedies for emotional burnout or to improve workplace performance and job satisfaction.

Using words like *workplace performance* and *job satisfaction* in connection with *mindfulness* is a danger signal. It would be repugnant to have key performance indicators for mindfulness as part of your annual job appraisal.

TURDUCKEN

If you don't know the word *turducken*, you should not be embarrassed. I didn't when I first stumbled upon it. And you may well share with me my first guess that it is vulgar. After all, it starts with *turd* and the second syllable isn't very promising either. *Turducken* sounds suspicious.

This goes to show how first impressions can mislead, even with words. *Turducken* is a food, and an Americanism, but not a fast-food Americanism. A *turducken* consists of a partly boned *TURkey*, into which a chef has inserted a boned *DUCK*, into which – this feels like the house that Jack built – the chef has inserted a boned *chickEN*. *TUR+DUCK+EN*.

The word *turducken*, linguistically speaking, is a blend or portmanteau word, like *advertainment* or *advertorial*, or *spork*, *motel*, *webinar*, *Spanglish* or Lewis Carroll's *chortle*.

Despite being new, and relatively uncommon in use, my spelling checker, somewhat surprisingly, doesn't mind *turducken*. But I think it's ugly. I'd be embarrassed to ask for it in a restaurant. (*Turducken à l'orange? Turducken Wellington? Pâté de foie turducken?*)

The only way I can see of rescuing *turducken* is to transport it properly into French, where its name would be something like *dincanoulet*. Now that sounds promising. I might just try that on the waiter next time I visit a restaurant.

Misuse and Disagreements

BILLION

Until 1974, the Americans and the British had different *billions*.

The British *billion* was a million millions, or 1 with 12 zeroes after it, or 10 to the power of 12 (10^{12}). The American *billion* was a thousand millions, or 1 with 9 zeroes after it, or 10 to the power of 9 (10^{9}).

It was a similar case with *trillion*, which was a million billions in England, and a thousand billions in America.

For a long time salaries were so low it didn't matter. But after a while billionaires wanted their real worth to be clearly known. And it was mathematically a lot easier to be a billionaire in America than in England.

In 1974, the Brits conceded defeat, sued for peace, ran the white flag up the numbers mast, and capitulated in the numbers war. Australia followed suit.

All the English-speaking world now follows the Americans, and a *billion* is a thousand million. And a *trillion* is a thousand billion (the old British billion, or 10^{12}). A *quadrillion* is a thousand trillion. And so on to infinity. The American billion carried the day.

GARBAGE, TRASH OR RUBBISH?

In Australia the Americans have much to answer for, such as the virtual demise of the useful word *rubbish*, which has been overrun by the imported *trash* and *garbage*.

Once upon a time, *rubbish* covered everything from waste paper to the remains of last Friday's prawns, which is an olfactory experience that escapes even from the protective shield of a plastic bag.

Nowadays we have to battle with three terms. *Rubbish* is disappearing, except in exclamations like 'That's rubbish!' And *rubbish man* is certainly outdated.

Trash seems to be used more generically, covering all kinds of things you want to throw away, especially on a computer. *Garbage* takes us back to the now-mummified prawns and other things you pick up only with rubber gloves.

Not everyone makes this crucial distinction. You can call someone trash, but probably not garbage. And what do we say for the removal of undesired material? 'The trash man cometh?' 'The garbage man is at the gate?'

Life was gentler with just *rubbish*. You can rubbish someone but they live on, damaged but extant. If you trash them they need medical or psychiatric attention.

TRUCKS AND LORRIES AND VANS

One of the more reliable tests for a recently arrived English person in Australia is their use of the word *lorry* instead of *truck*.

In the case of *trucks*, the Australians have followed the Americans, and our dictionaries list *lorry* as being British. We may understand it, in context, but we never use it to describe a large motor vehicle for transporting goods. There are *trucks* in Britain, but they are principally railway wagons. Interestingly, the original *truck* was a wheeled framework for mounting ships' guns. The motor vehicle meaning of *truck* dates from 1916.

And then there are *vans*. When is a vehicle a *truck*? When it isn't a *van*. *Vans* must have an enclosed goods space; a *truck* may.

If you are moving house and get a removalist company to come with muscle and a large vehicle, that's quite possibly a truck. If you hire a vehicle to do it yourself, and can use your ordinary driving licence, then it's probably a van. But then a small removalist company might have a van as well.

Truck has another idiomatic meaning. If you acquire goods through a less-than-transparent commercial transaction, you say that the goods *fell off the back of a truck*.

Perhaps this expression draws on our convict past. But then the phrase should be *fell off the back of a lorry*.

APARTMENT OR FLAT?

There was a time, a generation and a bit ago, when people who didn't live in houses lived in *flats*.

But no longer. Look at your Saturday paper in the accommodation column, or on any real estate website. Now it's all *apartments*. Which, like much else, we have taken from the Americans.

The word *apartment* comes via French from the Italian expression *a parte*, meaning 'apart' or 'separately', rather than living communally with lots of other relatives and hangers-on.

But what's the difference, since the word *flat* still exists in Australian English? An estate agent acquaintance told me that an apartment is a flat with a balcony, an ensuite and a jacuzzi.

So there you have it. The imported word has usurped the top end of the market, leaving our original *flat* to slum it.

SIDEWALK, NATURE STRIP AND FOOTPATH

What do you call the bit of land between your front fence and the road? Perhaps there's a *path*, or *footpath*, or *pavement* or an Americanised *sidewalk*. There can be bits of garden and grass. There may be grass but no concrete or asphalt to walk on. And, finally, there may be a *kerb* (at least in urban areas).

Pauline Bryant of the Australian National University surveyed this material in the late 1980s. Her results show that a sealed strip for walking on is a *footpath* everywhere in Australia, or sometimes a *pavement*.

If you have grass between your fence and the road, it's a *footpath* everywhere except in Western Australia, where they call it a *verge*. In Tasmania and Victoria, and somewhat over Victoria's borders to the north and west, it's a *nature strip*.

Canberra also has *nature strips*, perhaps because of the number of Melburnians who settled there. In Darwin they call it either a *footpath* or a *nature strip*.

Watch out for *nature strip*. It isn't what it sounds like to outsiders looking for places to strip off.

LOAN OR LEND?

Would you *loan* me five dollars? Are you having a *lend* of me?

The British and conservative view is that *loan* is a noun: you can make a loan, take a loan, default on a loan, reject a loan and generally negotiate a loan.

In contrast, *lend* is a verb: 'Please lend me that five dollars', or 'Friends, Romans, countrymen, lend me your ears'.

That narrow view, however, doesn't stand up entirely. Some of the freer usage is American, but only some of it.

Nowadays *loan* can certainly also be a verb: 'The lights were loaned to us by the theatre'.

And *lend* can be a noun, though usually colloquially or dialectally: 'Can I have a lend of your spanner?' And in the sense of trying something on, 'Are you having a lend of me?'

And do you remember Polonius in Shakespeare's *Hamlet*: 'Neither a borrower nor a lender be'?

JEALOUS AND ENVIOUS

Nowadays *jealous* and *envious* mean more or less the same thing: you want something that someone else has, so much that it can make you feel bad.

But originally *jealous* meant being protective of what you have. If you wanted to mean 'resentfully wanting something owned by someone else', you used *envious*.

Jealous has engulfed *envious*, so now we say, 'Don't be jealous of Annie's bike' if it's new and shiny and you really want it for yourself.

The original 'protective' meaning of *jealous* has more or less fallen off the perch. Though we still talk about *jealous husbands*. And you might hear the Speaker of a House of Parliament say, 'I am jealous for the good name of the House'.

So I used to be jealous of my perch and tried to keep you off. I was envious of your perch, and wanted to push you off. Now *jealous* does for both, and *envious* is on the skids.

SEWAGE AND SEWERAGE

Two words that are often confused are *sewage* and *sewerage*. Both words are derived from *sewer*, which tends to cause the confusion.

Sewage is the content, the effluent, the effluvia, the stuff we pump to the *sewage farm* for treatment. Farms normally grow things, of course, but not this sort. *Sewage* is a bit like electricity – it's the thing that travels down the wires or pipes.

Sewerage is the system of pipes and pumps that carries the *sewage* away from our houses, where we don't want to keep it, to the *sewage farm*. The *sewerage system* is like the electricity grid.

All clear? Perhaps not quite.

We too often hear people talking about the *sewage system*. Or people say they spread *sewerage* on the fields to make things grow. (Not unless a heap of pipework is good as fertiliser.)

On her 100th birthday, my grandma – this is a true story – was interviewed on radio 3AW in Melbourne. She was asked what social change had made the greatest impact in her long life. 'Sewerage, young man', she said to Derryn Hinch. And rightly so. The provision of piped sewerage changed the lives of many people. No more *night soil*. No more *night soil collectors* or *dunny men* to remove it. Reticulated sewerage – not sewage – systems have done a lot for public health.

I hope that, in the matter of *sewage* and *sewerage*, you are now clear about the content and the container.

RESPIRATORY

Winter is the time of flus and wheezes and sneezes and sniffs, and sniffles and wheezles, and general nasal dripping. It is also the time of bronchitis and pneumonia and other afflictions of the respiratory system.

Respiratory? Yes, if you please, *resPIratory*. Pronounced with four or five syllables, and with the stress on the second. Not *RESpuhTOry*. That doesn't even get close to the proper pronunciation, let alone the spelling. But that pronunciation is the dominant one in use today.

We know why people say *RESpuhTOry*. Part of the cause is the Americans again. They have a stress on the *o* in words like *mandatOry* and *obligatOry*.

But there's another reason. Having the English *r* twice in close proximity makes it hard to say. Because of the close *rs* in *respiRatoRy*, we drop one, as we do with *library* (*libry*) and *terrorism* (*terrism*).

That may be an explanation for *RESpuhTOry*, but it's no excuse. If you value your respiratory system, talk about it properly. Respect your respiration.

DEMUR AND DEMURE

There are pairs of words in English that are almost identical in spelling and/or pronunciation, and that are landmines for speakers looking for mistakes to make.

Loath and *loathe* belong here, and are often and embarrassingly confused, much to the hilarity of those who can remember which is which. I am loath to admit that I loathe sentimental novels.

Another, and probably less familiar, pair is *demure* and *demur*.

Demure means modest, reserved and shy, and is mostly used to describe women. In manuals of etiquette, being *demure* used to be a very desirable and necessary quality of 'proper' young ladies.

Demur means to object or to show reluctance. As in, 'He would normally have agreed without question, but on this occasion he demurred'. And it can be a noun: 'He conceded the point without demur'.

If you are demure you may well demur, though there must be ways of demurring without being at all demure.

Come to think of it, isn't it simpler to *object modestly*?

RAPID COFFEE

If you want to show you are an ignorant parvenu, ask the barista in your favourite coffee shop for an *eXpresso*.

The Italian word is *eSpresso*. The English prefix *ex-* is *es-* in Italian. For example, English *extreme* is Italian *estremo*, English *exclaim* is Italian *esclamare*, and so on.

So, if you really know your *macchiato* from your *marocchino*, and your *stretto* from your *corretto*, do ask for an *espresso*. Perhaps *espresso con panna*, which will give the barista a moment of panic if their Italian is worse than yours. Smile benignly and be indulgent, and just a little superior. And with an arched eyebrow suggest that you hope that this coffee shop is indeed one that can comprehend, and provide, an *espresso con panna*.

If they don't know what *panna* means (for those in strife and unable to order their coffee, Italian *panna* means cream), maybe you should play it safe and change your order to a *latte*. Or change your coffee shop.

ESPRESSO

'HOME IN ON' OR 'HONE IN ON'?

We usually have little trouble in using *home* and *hone* as verbs. We *hone* or sharpen a knife. Pigeons *home*, or find their way home, as in a *homing pigeon*. In a less friendly way, missiles *home* and explode, and we can *home* animals to help out the RSPCA (and the animals).

But *home in on* and *hone in on* give rise to much stress, uncertainty and, frankly, error. The two sounds *m* and *n*, said on their own, sound rather similar in noisy or lo-fi environments. They are nasal sounds, because when you pronounce them the air comes out of your nose. If you don't believe me, try holding your nose and saying these sounds. Stop before you explode.

If we want to say that something locates a point to direct itself to, then it's looking for a *home*, and we should *home in on* something with an *m*. As do the pigeons. There's no idea of sharpening or honing.

Homing in on something also works for ideas and abstracts: 'Give him a bit more time and he'll home in on a way of solving that'.

If he doesn't, he obviously needs to hone his skills.

REMUNERATION AND RENUMERATION

Two more words that commonly confuse *m* and *n*, especially in pronunciation, are *remuneration* (your salary or wage) and *renumeration* (the act of enumerating or counting something again).

Part of the difficulty involves the sounds *m* and *n*, and distinguishing them reliably, which happens, as we have just seen, with *home* and *hone*.

In addition, *remuneration* is relatively uncommon and *renumeration* is downright rare.

Confusing them has become so entrenched that the *Oxford English Dictionary* actually lists *renumeration* as a variant of *remuneration*. But it's marginal at best. *Renumeration* is *re* + *numeration*, or counting something again. *Remuneration* comes from Latin and means 'to be recompensed'.

It's still important to remember to renumerate your remuneration – to count and re-count your pay – and not to remunerate your renumeration, which is to make a payout for counting something again. If you want to be paid at all, that is.

EXASPERATE AND EXACERBATE

Among the pairs of similar-sounding words that cause us grief and sometimes embarrassment, *exasperate* and *exacerbate* merit an honourable mention.

Exasperate means to drive someone to distraction, frustration and anger: 'He exasperated me beyond the limits of human endurance'. It comes from the Latin *asper*, meaning 'rough'. Think of the related word *asperity*.

In contrast, *exacerbate* is derived from the Latin *acerbus*, meaning 'harsh' or 'bitter', and *acer*, meaning 'sharp, severe, fierce'. So *exacerbate* means 'to make things worse': 'What he did exacerbated the situation'.

In these words, we have two sources of confusion: the common negative meaning of an unfavourable outcome, and the close similarity of pronunciation. I've heard people say both 'I'm so exacerbated at her' and 'What he did has exasperated the situation'. And both were wrong.

One useful way to sort them out is this: generally speaking, you exasperate people and exacerbate situations.

If you aren't certain of the difference, it's prudent to be considerate and avoid doing either.

DECIMATE

In Latin the word *decem* means 'ten' and the word *decimate* means 'to take a tenth of'. In Ancient Rome, the army generals had an amiable strategy. If one of their legions wasn't fighting hard enough in battle they would slaughter 10 per cent of their own troops and send the remaining 90 per cent back into battle to try harder.

In modern English we are massacring the word *decimate*. Some people think it means to slaughter 90 per cent and keep 10 per cent, which would probably not work well in a battle situation.

Others – the vast majority – think it means 'to obliterate', 'to win massively' or 'to wipe the opposition away'. Sports commentators love decimating things: 'We absolutely decimated the opposition today'.

It's probably too late to save the proper *decimate*. If you use it in the older sense you may well be misunderstood. But be wary when you hear it, just in case the user really knows what it means. Maybe the commentator only obliterated 10 per cent of the other team after all.

FORFEND

In English we have several words ending in *-fend*, like *defend* and *offend*. They come from a Latin verb *fendere*, meaning, among other things, 'to push'. Think of *fend off*.

We also have *forfend*, meaning 'prevent' or 'protect'. *Forfend* is rarely used, but I was reminded of it recently by a colleague who said: 'We have defence and offence, why not forfence?'

Forfence doesn't get into the *Oxford English Dictionary*, so it doesn't exist officially. And the most common phrase with *forfend* nowadays is *heaven forfend*, meaning 'heaven forbid'. Variants are *the gods forfend* and *God forfend*, and, very occasionally, *the saints forfend*.

It's a useful, powerful phrase. Heaven forfend that I ever run out of Vegemite™.

LITERALLY 'LITERALLY'

Literally means 'exactly, to the letter'. If you ended a relationship more brutally than you intended, you might say, 'I told him I would be happy to see him dead, but I didn't mean him to take that literally'.

But of late *literally* has become very common to add emphasis, with some strange results if you do take *literally* in the literal sense. For instance, a friend reported that a book she had just finished literally broke her heart. I don't want to die yet, and so I will avoid that book at all costs.

'Jim literally doesn't have a brain in his head.' Better call the neurosurgeon. 'He shouldn't have said that: he's literally shot himself in the foot.' Better call an ambulance. 'He got home after 2.00 am, and he's literally in the poo.' Better call the gardener. Or a sewage engineer.

Misusing *literally* in this way is like saying *really*. But it IS a misuse. 'I really don't have the stomach for that' is fine, as it means I'm not up to it. But 'I literally don't have the stomach for that' means, strictly speaking, that you are missing part of your digestive system. The result is the same as if it 'literally broke my heart'. Both are terminal.

UNIQUE

Absolutely unique beachfront!!! shrieks a real estate agent's billboard.

A completely unique experience, oozes a travel brochure.

'Each model has her very unique style,' says a fashion reporter.

Unique comes from the Latin *unus*, meaning 'one'. *Unique*, strictly speaking, means 'one of a kind'. We are each of us unique. By definition.

But alas, *unique* has lost its modesty and gone on the town. The wrong end of town. It now means something like 'absolutely, totally, extremely remarkable'.

Usage ultimately wins. Language is like that, and it's hard to push back against a change with a good head of steam up. But this one makes me cringe and writhe. And I twitch, visibly and sometimes audibly, when I hear it.

INFER AND IMPLY

Two more words that tend to trip over each other's feet are *infer* and *imply*.

For many people they mean the same, especially when we say, 'What are you inferring?' If that is intended to say, 'What are you trying to suggest?', it's wrong.

Imply and *infer* are in fact mirror images of each other.

If I want to suggest something in what I say, I *imply* it. If you want to read something into what I have said, you *infer* it.

So I may imply something and you may not infer anything if you don't get it. Or I can say something quite innocent and you may infer all kinds of devious intentions.

Be careful with *implying* and *inferring*. Remember: the speaker implies, the hearer infers.

DISORDER OR DISEASE?

You may panic if your doctor says you have a disease, but how should you react if you are told that you have a disorder?

Both *disease* and *disorder* are different from physical injury – a broken leg is not a disease. Beyond that, however, these two words have a fuzzy area between them.

A *disease* is a defined way of being sick: some part of your body is not working the way it should because of a virus or a bacterium or a dysfunction, like coronary disease. There will be detectable symptoms. There is a change or damage to your physical self.

A *disorder* is less specific, and usually doesn't involve an observable change or damage in the same way as a disease. Function may be affected, but the effects of a disorder may not be so easily seen.

Best of all, aspire to neither.

JETTY AND PIER

Some of our words have specific meanings to people who know them. People who don't know mangle them, and use them indiscriminately and badly, to the anguish of the people who do know.

Two such words are *jetty* and *pier*, not to mention *wharf* and *quay*.

Lesson number one: a *jetty* and a *pier* jut out from the shore and extend into the water, be it sea or lake, or even river. In contrast, a *wharf* and a *quay* are parallel to the shore.

Lesson number two: a *wharf* and a *pier* are built on piles, while a *jetty* and a *quay* are built on fill. You can't fish under the latter two, or paddle a canoe under them, or float under them on your floaties. They are solid.

So there you have it. Simple and comprehensive. You may now sally forth and confound your nautical and piscatorial* friends with your new-found knowledge.

---

* Did I hear you ask about *piscatorial*? That word has to do with people who fish, or fishers, as they are now known. Or just conceivably *fisherpersons*.

SPITTING IMAGE

Among the many odd idioms in English, *spitting image* is one of the stranger ones. Why should we need to spit in order to confirm similarity?

It turns out that even our best dictionaries aren't sure why. One suggestion is that it is a corruption of *split* – when you split timber and put the faces together, as when making the back of a violin. For understandable reasons, that is called *fiddleback,* but it doesn't solve our problem of spitting.

For *spitting image*, there is one quotation from the seventeenth century involving a child being so like his father *as if he were spit out of his mouth*. In the following centuries, we find phrases like *the very spit of*, meaning 'very similar'. How all this came about remains a mystery.

But spitting does have cultural value, in a manner of speaking. Spitting on the ground can imply disrespect (though not if you are a footballer in the middle of a match), and spitting in someone's face expresses contempt.

But spitting used to be socially acceptable. I can remember – just – that railway carriages used to have a *spittoon* to collect the output of spitting. And a more genteel receptacle for spitting was called a *cuspidor*. There also used to be a *spit handshake*, when men would spit on their hands before shaking hands as a special sign of honesty and commitment.

Times have certainly changed. And happily so.

ASSUME AND PRESUME

Assume and *presume* are two words that are fairly close in sound, and close enough in meaning to cause confusion. I am particularly interested in these two verbs followed by the word *that*: *to assume that* and *to presume that.**

If you *assume* that something is going to happen, you have no data, no evidence, no proof and you are adopting a hopeful expectation with no specific substance behind it. If I say, 'I assume that he'll remember to bring the champagne', I am uttering a pious hope, especially if it has been my job to remember the champagne and I forgot it.

On the other hand, if you *presume* that something is going to be done, then you have some information and basis for expecting things to happen. As I introduce a colleague to a visitor, and they are both specialists in the same field, I might say, 'I presume that you two know about each other's work already'. The fact that they are in the same field of research gives me reason for my belief. If I say, 'I assume that you know each other's work', it can almost be rude. Well, it could, to people who care for such distinctions.

There you have it. You assume that something will happen without proof, and you presume something will happen if you actually have some reason to think so.

---

* This only works if *assume* and *presume* are followed by *that* or a clause. *Assuming* the mantle of power, or *assuming* an expression of irritation, are quite different. And if you *presume* to do something, or *presume* on someone, you are being arrogant and imposing without consideration or care. Come to think of it, that is what I do to you, hapless readers.

ACUTE AND CHRONIC

Acute and *chronic* can both mean 'severe': 'There was an acute/chronic shortage of prawns, which placed a significant strain on the restaurant industry'. But *chronic* can have an additional meaning of persisting or continuing over time.

This leads to a special case where the two words need to be clearly distinguished, which is in talking about pain.

Acute pain comes on fairly suddenly and is usually caused by a wound, infection or trauma. You can have acute pain from a cut or a bruise, a broken bone, or an infected tooth. You fix the cause and the acute pain should go away.

In contrast, *chronic pain* is pain that has been present for a longer time. One common definition for *chronic pain* is pain that has lasted all day for three months out of the last six. People with chronic pain often don't have a clear cause for the pain, so it's much harder to treat. There are many people who live with chronic pain. It would be easier to treat if the pain were acute, when a pill or an injection, or some intervention, should fix it.

Acute pain may hurt, but there's a better chance that it might be easily remedied.

HYPERTHERMIA AND HYPOTHERMIA

Unless we make a special effort to differentiate between *hyperthermia* and *hypothermia* in pronunciation, these two medically important words sound the same in English. However, they mean totally different things, and both are potentially fatal, so we'd better work out which is which.

The more common one is *hypOthermia*. This condition occurs when your internal body temperature falls significantly, or dangerously, below the normal range (37 degrees Celsius or 98.6 degrees Fahrenheit). *HypOthermia* is when people are exposed to cold, for instance in water or in wintry weather.

Less commonly heard is *hypERthermia*. This is when your body temperature is significantly above the norm, and you overheat, and is a condition that mostly occurs in deserts and on hot summer days.

There is no problem with the written forms, which are clearly different. The problem is with the pronunciation. The second syllable in both *hypothermia* and *hyperthermia* is not stressed – that honour goes to the *-therm-*. Being unstressed, they both tend to be pronounced with the neutral schwa* vowel.

In practice, it's usually clear which is meant, and so which kind of medical attention is needed. Medical practitioners communicate about these terms entirely clearly. But, if there's a remote chance of misinterpretation, you can always pronounce the vowel in full in order to distinguish them. That way no-one gets the wrong medical attention.

How to remember which is which? Well, *e* is earlier in the alphabet than *o*; it's higher in the list, and so hypERthermia is higher on a thermometer than hypOthermia.

---

* Schwa (pronounced shwa) is the name linguists give to the unstressed vowel at the start of *about* or the end of *comma*. It's the most common vowel in English, since we have so many unstressed vowels, and we spell it in many different ways. Linguists write it as ə.

CEMENT AND CONCRETE

Out of the two words *cement* and *concrete*, which is the powder and which is the solid?

The correct answer is that *cement* is the powder. You mix it with water, sand and stones, also known as aggregate, and it sets solid to make *concrete* (unless, that is, you have put in too much water, in which case you end up with a sloppy slurry).

Some people use the word *cement* to mean the same as *concrete*. They say, 'I have a cement driveway'. The word *cement* can also be a verb: both in the concrete sense (pardon the pun) of cementing something into place, or in the metaphorical sense of people getting married and cementing their relationship.

There's also a popular expression that uses *cement* in this fundamentally incorrect way. I am a bit of a motor mouth. My colleagues at the ABC kindly say that I can *talk under wet cement*. If we were talking about cement the powder, it would not be wet and I would suffocate. But, as it is, I babble and bubble on, wet concrete not withstanding. And will perhaps eventually still suffocate.

ADVERSE AND AVERSE

Another pair of words in English that are close in spelling and pronunciation, but significantly different in meaning and usage, is *adverse* and *averse*.

Adverse conditions are unfavourable, harmful or otherwise stop you achieving what you want to do. *Adverse weather* can prevent the start of a yacht race, or the harvesting of wine grapes. *Adverse conditions* can also include natural disasters like earthquakes.

People are not usually *adverse*.

In contrast, *averse* is almost only used after the verb *to be*, and refers pretty well only to people. If you are *averse to something* you don't like it or you oppose it. You can be averse to sharing your feelings, discussing politics, violence, mosquitoes, or admitting to a passion for tiddlywinks.

Put like that, *adverse* and *averse* are clearly distinct. But in everyday usage many people are not averse to getting them confused.

FLOUT AND FLAUNT

You'd better be clear what you want to *flaunt* and what you want to *flout*. Otherwise you could find yourself in some odd situations, including jail, if you try to *flout* the rules about drinking and driving. You won't get far if you try to *flaunt* them either, but the consequences are very different.

If you *flaunt* something you show it off, especially if you want to make someone envious or to be deliberately defiant. I can flaunt clothes, a new car, a new house, shoes, jewellery or a new bassoon. Though how you might flaunt a new bassoon is open to question. Perhaps by playing music like 'The Elephant and the Flea'.

Flout, on the other hand, means to disobey, especially to do it obviously. You can *flout convention* by turning up to a wedding in a swimsuit, or by singing rude songs at the Olympic Opening Ceremony. Flouting is risky, since you are saying, in effect, 'I don't care. This is what I want to do'.

If you *flaunt some outrageous behaviour*, you can simultaneously *flout convention*. That's where the two words can get confused. If you are confused, give up both flaunting and flouting. It's safer that way.

ALTERNATELY AND ALTERNATIVELY

What is the difference between *alternately* and *alternatively*? In Latin, *alter* means 'the other of two', so *to alternate* is to do the other thing of a set of two. You *alternate* between A and B.

Alternately picks up on this idea of 'the other of two'. If I like shiraz and grenache, I might drink them alternately, one after the other.

Alternatively means to do something different. If I try shiraz and grenache and don't like either, I might say, 'Alternatively, I could try beer or cider or vodka'.

However, especially in the United States, *alternate* and *alternately* can also be used in this 'other' sense without restricting it to two. You can have an alternate choice among hundreds, and you can decide alternately to do that. This usage is not officially recommended among Australians – or among the British – but like many Americanisms it is gaining traction.

I'm going to stop there. Alternatively or alternately, I might not stop at all.

COMPOSE AND COMPRISE

Speakers of English often get their undergarments in torsion – aka their knickers in a twist – over the difference between *compose* and *comprise*. And so they should. Knickers are barely enough to cover the terrible things done to these two words.

Comprise means 'to be made up of' or 'to include'. So we can say, 'The state comprises three distinct regions: a desert region, a tropical region and a temperate region'.

If you want to use the word *compose* to capture this meaning, you need to frame it in the passive voice: 'The state is composed of three distinct regions: a desert region, a tropical region and a temperate region'.

Unfortunately, *comprise* and *compose* are getting themselves badly confused.

Some people say, 'The state comprises of three distinct regions', or 'The state is comprised of three distinct regions'. Our dictionaries note this misuse, but they don't tut-tut over it loudly enough. *Comprise* and *compose* are too close for security, and need some help in prising themselves apart.

BRACES AND SUSPENDERS

What do you use to stop your trousers from falling down? I am not referring to elastic, nor yet to a belt, but to straps that go over the shoulders and stop the trousers descending to the area of immodesty.

We used to call these things *braces*. The word is related to French and the term *embrace*, meaning 'to fold something securely in one's arms'. There are other kinds of modern braces that hold things in place, like tooth braces for orthodontistry, and bracing pieces of iron or timber used in carpentry. The word *braces* for trousers was only used in the plural – you could not wear a *brace* to hold your trousers up.

But in Australia at least 20 years ago, give or take, the word *braces* started to be threatened by the American word *suspenders*. In Australia the term *suspender*, which could be singular, used to refer to a belt worn by women to hold their stockings up. Men, when I were a lad, wore braces, not suspenders.

Nowadays we do not support our trousers very often in this way, and people who do tend to do so without a jacket, as a kind of signature vestment. And when people try to insulate their trousers from gravity, we increasingly use the American word *suspenders*. My Australian dictionaries list the device for supporting trousers as second choice under *suspender*. My impression is that it probably merits first billing nowadays. Particularly now that women wear suspenders much less than they used to. Thank pantyhose for their demise.

If your suspenders and braces are all in place, you should be modestly dressed, regardless of your gender.

EMIGRATION AND IMMIGRATION

Speakers of English sometimes get confused when they try to write *emigrate* and *immigrate*, or *emigration* and *immigration*. Part of the problem is that the stress is usually on the *-grate* or *-ation*, and that means that the start of the word is pronounced indistinctly, and both words come out sounding pretty much the same.

Fear not. Help is at hand, and the answer is simple.

Emigration comes from Latin, in which either *e-* or *ex-* at the start of words like *expatriate* and *exit* means 'going out'. This meaning is characteristic of hundreds of words in English that we have borrowed from Latin and involve going out of a place or away from it. Pick up a decent-sized dictionary and look for words starting with the prefix *ex-*.

Immigration goes in the other direction. It starts with *im-*, and that is a variant of the Latin prefix and preposition *in*. In Latin, that means 'in' or 'into'.

All that is consistent with the difference between *explosion* and *implosion*. An *explosion* goes outwards, and an *implosion* goes inwards.

And that's it! Emigrants leave the country, and immigrants come into it.

COMPLIMENT AND COMPLEMENT

Another two words that are commonly confused between the *i* and *e* spellings are *compliment* and *complement*. In speaking there is no difference because the middle vowel is unstressed; they sound the same, unless we deliberately pronounce them differently.

But when we write them we need to be clear which one we have in mind.

Compliment with an *i* means to say nice things about someone or something, to be approving. A courteous person will compliment their date's hair, dress, demeanour and style.

Complement with an *e* means to add something to make it complete, or to provide something that balances and makes whatever you are talking about more satisfying and whole. A well-chosen pair of shoes may complement an outfit, or a judicious strategy may complement one that is otherwise incomplete.

You can get yourself into unseemly tangles if you choose the wrong one, and you expose yourself to the scorn of people who claim to know their *i* from their *e*. As a general rule, you compliment people with an *i*, but you complement things and abstracts with an *e*.

TENDED MY RESIGNATION

Online posts are hotbeds of language misuse. We have all done it. Predictive spelling has a wild stab in the dark at what it thinks we might be writing, and we accept – or just trust and don't check – and post our errors for the world to see.

Politicians and other public figures can't escape this modern misuse. In one case, a former premier (or perhaps a member of his staff) tweeted that he had *tended* his resignation. The Governor promptly, and correctly, replied that he had accepted the *tendered* resignation.

The trouble is that the way we pronounce English makes *tended* and *tendered* sound the same in the past tense: 'He tended to believe me' and 'He tendered his resignation'.

The same thing has happened with *chat* and *chatter*: 'He chatted to his friends' and 'He chattered incessantly'. *To chat* is to talk informally. *To chatter* is to talk a lot and often inconsequentially.

If you are American, or Canadian, or Irish, or from

many parts of rural England, you pronounce the *r* in *tender* and *chatter* and all is clear: *tended* is not the same as *tendered*, and *chatted* is clearly not *chattered*. But Australians, along with Kiwis and most metropolitan British, don't pronounce *r* after vowels.

So we have to live with uncertainty about whether someone has *chatted* or *chattered*. Unless we make the vowel in *chattERed* unnaturally and uncomfortably long. But we really do need to know when to write *tended* and *tendered*.

PROVED AND PROVEN

Should you say *proved* or *proven*? Both are heard, and read, in the English we encounter every day.

If you take the verb *to prove*, which means to demonstrate the validity or viability of something, then the simple past tense is *proved*: 'He proved the theorem' and 'She proved him wrong'.

If you want to use the past tense of *prove* with *have*, you may use either *proved* or *proven*. *Proved* is more common in Britain and the Commonwealth countries, and *proven* is more common in America and is standard in Scottish English: 'We have proved/proven that this approach isn't going to work'.

Both *proved* and *proven* have roots deep in the history of English, though *proven* has enjoyed a resurgence over the last century or so.

If you like reading American detective fiction, and there is a lot of excellent writing of this type around, you may well encounter *proven* more than *proved*. There is also the idiom *innocent until proven guilty*.

However, if you want to use an adjective, the only

choice is *proven*: a *proven remedy*, a *proven technique* to learn new vocabulary. The truth of this theory is *proven*. There is no *proved remedy*.

Proven can only be used when you are demonstrating the truth of something. If you are causing bread to rise through the action of yeast, you have proved the bread, or the bread has proved over two hours.

ENSURE AND INSURE

Pairs of verbs that differ just in one letter cause a great deal of confusion in spoken and written English. Examples like *effect* with an *e* and *affect* with an *a* cause ordinarily decisive people to suffer from indecision.

Happily, there are a few we can resolve more simply. One of those pairs is *insure* with an *i* and *ensure* with an *e*.

If you want to pay a company to cover you against loss, damage or accident, the sort of thing that Lloyd's of London became famous for, then that is *insure* with an *i*. *Insure* with an *i* can also be used in a more general sense of 'protect against': 'They wanted to insure themselves against further marital disasters'.

Your *insurance policy* has an *i*. There is no *ENsurance policy*. You should turn away from your door any representative who tries to sell you one.

For everything else, including many expressions when you want to make something sure (and *insure* and *ensure* come from the Latin *securus*, meaning 'free from care'), *ensure* with an *e* is more common:

'This initiative will ensure that we end up with a profit at the end of the year'.

The Americans, though, have some tendency to use the *i* form in legal language: 'We need to insure that he'll be in court'.

I hope all that ensures your ongoing peace – not piece – of mind.

QUOTE AND QUOTATION, INVITE AND INVITATION

English has a talent for turning a word into another part of speech without altering it. This is called conversion. One fairly recent example of conversion involves the word *quote*.

Once upon a time, if you quoted something, that was called a *quotation*. At school I was encouraged to support my arguments in essays with quotations. I was expected to quote.

But nowadays we often hear *quote* used as a noun: 'That was a great quote', or 'You need another quote to make that point properly', or 'Has the builder submitted his quote yet?' The word *quote* is exactly the same in all these cases, it's just that the verb is now being used also as a noun. And the older and longer word *quotation* is starting to find itself under threat. Conversion works like that, generally to the detriment of longer words.

Now let's look at another, slightly more involved, example.

Do you send someone an *invite* or an *invitation* to the soirée that you are planning next weekend?

Until reasonably recently you would *inVITE* someone to your soirée by sending them an *invitation*. Nowadays you can send an *INvite*. A number of people, me included, don't much like receiving an *INvite*. But we recognise what it is trying to do and respond accordingly.

Just be aware that the stress has shifted from the last syllable to the first syllable: when you *inVITE* someone you send them an *INvite*. So it's not pure conversion, but conversion with a shift of stress. The same thing used to happen if you wished to *exPORT* some *EXports*.

CLIENTS OR GUESTS OR PASSENGERS OR PATIENTS?

There was a time when you knew where you were when you paid for professional services.

If you went to the doctor or the dentist you were a *patient*.

If you paid your lawyer or your accountant you were a *client*.

If you visited someone and enjoyed their hospitality, no payment involved, you were a *guest*.

But all that has changed.

First, *patients* are out. Some doctors and dentists now have not patients but *clients*. I know that the Latin word behind *patient* means 'to suffer passively'. But if you take away the suffering component, I am quite happy to be passive with my doctor and dentist. They have the expertise and I want them to apply it to me to make me better.

Second, airlines now tell me I am not a *passenger* but a *guest*. I like this even less, and that includes when they invite me to *enjoy their hospitality*. Hospitality – shmospitality. I have paid for it, and I expect it to be provided. I am not a guest. And the service they provide has little to do with welcoming outsiders into their home and providing them, as a host should, with food and drink.

What's wrong with *patients* and *passengers*? Maybe we can swap them round. If you think a healthcare service is taking you for a ride, present yourself as a *passenger*. And if your airline insists on calling you a *guest*, ask if their *hospitality* will be free of charge.

VOMITORIUM

A *vomitorium*, in popular understanding, is a room where the Ancient Romans used to go to throw up, so that they could go back and indulge in even more eating at whichever banquet they were attending.

The origin of *vomitorium* looks plausible. The Latin verb for 'to vomit' was *vomo*, and there was another form, *vomito*, meaning to chunder often and copiously. Hence, the argument goes, is the origin of *vomitorium*.

But this is a mistake. Yes, the Ancient Romans did go in for binge eating and drinking, but they didn't practise emesis in a *vomitorium*. Their Ancient Roman technicolour yawn, if and when it happened, was elsewhere.

No, a *vomitorium* was a passage in buildings like the Ancient Roman circus. It was designed to get large numbers of spectators into and out of the circus in a hurry. The flood of Ancient Romans, anxious to see slaves being disembowelled by lions and other jolly sights, disgorged en masse into or out of their seats. The only vomiting was a metaphor, of people and crowds.

I have, however, heard of a room used for practising emesis. It is called a *chunderium*. I haven't yet found the Latin verb from which it derives, but I'm in hot pursuit.

BAITED BREATH

Consider *bated breath* and *baited breath*. Not bad breath or dragon breath, aka halitosis. Just breath. And in particular how we bate it.

There's only one phrase in English that combines those words, and that's *bated breath*. Not *baited breath* – you don't put something on your breath to attract game fish.

Up to the sixteenth century there was an English verb *to bate*, which meant 'to restrain'. We know it in the modern verb *to abate*, which means 'to become less intense', as in 'the wind abated'.

So if you bate your breath you are restraining it or holding it, waiting for something to be resolved. It's a moment of suspension. Not at all like putting mullet guts on a rusty fishhook.

CARPE DIEM

A few years ago, the American writer Stephen Marche reminded us that the scriptwriters in the film *Dead Poets' Society* got something rather wrong. The Latin phrase *carpe diem* does not mean 'seize the day'. That sounds like grabbing something firmly with both hands and squeezing it tight.

Carpe diem is actually less violent and more reflective. It means something like 'pluck the day and cherish it'. The verb *carpo* is used to pick, enjoy or gather flowers, fruits and plants. And, as you do it, pause to consider their shape, charm and meaning. That's what the Latin poet Horace meant. Not at all like the vigorous adolescent seizing that was practised in that otherwise admirable film.

A LAST WORD…

The English language is currently going through a period of tremendous ferment, growth and expansion. This is happening around the globe, not only in the Anglosphere, but also in countries where English is a second language. Old 'rules' are being challenged, or weakened. New ones are emerging. Novel words, expressions and meanings are being created and spread with all the speed that the internet can provide. Keeping track of all this is a daunting task.

One excellent medium is through talkback radio.

Being involved in a weekly half-hour language talkback radio program for 23 years has taught me a lot. I have thoroughly enjoyed talking on air to thousands of people whom I would never have met otherwise. And I have collected, and discussed, and argued about, and mused on, mountains of bits of language and listeners' views on them. These listeners are people who care about language, and have a wealth of personal knowledge and experience. Talkback radio gives them a channel to explore it.

The Queensland ABC Radio programs are podcast and have a worldwide audience. To find the podcasts, open the Podcast application on a mobile device and type:

Roly Sussex

Alternatively, point your browser to:

podcasts.apple.com/au/podcast/a-word-in-your-ear/id336052520

If you'd like to join in the discussion about our changing language, go to the Facebook page @rolysussex. You can also join the closed email list called Langtalk-L on language by emailing r.sussex@uq.edu.au.

You too can contribute to discovering what is happening to English, especially – but not only – in Australia.

ACKNOWLEDGEMENTS

'No man is an island.' Neither is a book. John Donne, having written the former, would have appreciated the latter no less. This book would not have happened without a great deal of support. I have much pleasure in thanking the people responsible.

First, my colleagues and friends in radio at the Australian Broadcasting Corporation, where I have been doing half-hour talkback radio programs every week for nearly a quarter of a century. And most particularly Kelly Higgins-Devine, my presenter at ABC Brisbane for a number of years. It was she who suggested the whole idea of the woofties, and who planned and implemented the way they would be used on radio. The woofties, as they developed, bear the imprint of her quick understanding and infectious good humour.

The woofties also show the unmistakable influence of my producer from the ABC Brisbane promos studio, Geoff Cavanagh. What Geoff doesn't know about voice and audio isn't worth recording. His job is to critique my texts, to cajole me into producing high-quality recorded audio, and then to massage the results into a form usable on radio. His judgement about language and recording is infallible, and I have learnt much from working with him.

Over the years I have also benefited tremendously from the verbal and personal company of my many presenters – people like Richard Fidler, Kelly Higgins-Devine, Carole Whitelock and Peter Goers. They will find echoes of their talk in this book as well. And so will the tens of thousands of listeners to 'A Word in Your Ear', people in Australia and (through streaming and podcasts) overseas whom I have met through the medium of radio and whose opinions, data and judgements about language have enriched my thinking.

And then I had the good fortune to find the University of Queensland Press to publish the book. My editor, Felicity Dunning, has an exquisite sense for content, structure, prose and nuance, and her influence on the shape and execution of this book is everywhere. The experience, energy, good humour and judgement of my publisher, Madonna Duffy, have been invaluable. Jo Hunt did a splendid job of the design, and Kate McCormack made sure that we were legal.

And John Eyley has caught the tone – and seriousness – of the book's contents, and has created outstanding original drawings.

It has been a distinct pleasure and a rewarding experience to work with you all.

As an incurably non-island person I couldn't have done this book without special people: Bogna, Matthew, Asia and Susan. They have lovingly and steadfastly sustained and inspired me through the many phases of this project, and have helped to keep me on song and in song.

Finally, my thanks to the English language in Australia, in all its teenage testosterone turbulence and strength and springy vitality: from moment to moment shifting from being like polished furniture to a thermal mud pool, to the broad expanse of a river in flood, to a volcano in eruption, to a surf beach during a storm, to a sputtering camp fire, and to a stunning incarnadine sunset in Far North Queensland.

Omnibus gratias ago.

LIST OF ENTRIES

Misuse and Disagreements